the HOUSE BOOK

MURDOCH

First published in 2006 by Murdoch Books Pty Limited

Murdoch Books Pty Limited Australia
Pier 8/9, 23 Hickson Road
Sydney NSW 2000
Phone: 61 (02) 8220 2000
Fax: 61 (02) 8220 2558
www.murdochbooks.com.au

Murdoch Books UK Limited
Erico House, 6th Floor North
93/99 Upper Richmond Road
Putney, London SW15 2TG
Phone: + 44 (0) 20 8785 5995
Fax: + 44 (0) 20 8785 5985

Chief Executive: Juliet Rogers
Publisher: Kay Scarlett
Design Manager: Vivien Valk
Design and illustrations: Alex Frampton
Editor: Ariana Klepac
Production: Monika Paratore

Text: Toby Buckland, Scott Cam, Julian Cassell, Greg Cheetham, Michael Clark,
Mark Corke, Len Crane, Jane Davies, Mark Edwards, Frank Gardner, Lulu Grimes,
Kay Halsey, Alison Haynes, Ariana Klepac, Catherine Lawrence, Mike Lawrence,
Chris Maton, Peter Parham, Nerys Purchon, Kim Rowney, Richard Rutherford,
John Street, Kevin Tenney

Printed by Midas Printing (Asia) Ltd
Printed in China

National Library of Australia Cataloguing-in-Publication Data:
The House book : thousands of practical tips for cleaning,
repairing and organizing your home. Includes index.
ISBN 978 1 74045 792 7.
ISBN 1 74045 792 7.

1. Home economics - Handbooks, manuals, etc. 2. Storage in the home - Handbooks,
manuals, etc. 3. Cleaning - Handbooks, manuals, etc. 4. Buildings - Repair and
reconstruction - Handbooks, manuals, etc. 640

NOTE: In some areas it may not be legal to carry out even simple plumbing or
electrical tasks, so ensure you check this before beginning any home repair jobs.

the
HOUSE
BOOK

Thousands of practical tips for cleaning, repairing and organizing your home

contents

outside

Clever outdoor housekeeping and maintenance makes sense on health, aesthetic and environmental grounds. Also, if you get into a routine of regular outdoor cleaning, you will come across jobs that you can attend to before they become major problems. The following pages provide ideas for all manner of outdoor maintenance including cleaning, painting tips, caring for furniture and outdoor features, as well as guidance on how to organize the garden shed.

The ideal garden

A carefully planned garden is an enticing haven for its inhabitants as well as environmentally friendly. Here are a few general tips to consider:

- Shrubs around the house will have a cooling effect on your home since plants don't absorb and retain heat as much as concrete.

- Trees will provide shade, and act as a windbreak and noise and air filter.

- Deciduous trees near north-facing windows in the southern hemisphere (and south-facing in the northern hemisphere), allow the maximum amount of sun in the winter when the branches are bare. In the summer they provide shade.

- Pergolas and trellises covered in trailing, deciduous vines add shade in the summer while allowing light through in the winter.

- Native bushes between the house and road absorb noise and fumes as well as attract native birds to the garden.

- A compost heap and worm farm are used to recycle biodegradable household waste and garden clippings into a natural fertilizer and mulch that can be put back into the garden.

- Mulch is used on garden beds to maximize water retention and to suppress weeds.

- A rainwater tank augments the local water supply.

- Grey water is channelled onto the lawn rather than wasted.

- A fixed watering system delivers water directly to where it is needed without wasteful run-off.

- A small kitchen garden provides an abundant supply of fresh herbs and salad vegetables.

- Companion planting helps to deter troublesome garden pests without the use of chemicals.

THE MAILBOX

■ For safety reasons, never put your name on the mailbox. If you want to identify it in some way, just use your initials.

■ Position the mailbox clearly on the boundary of your property.

■ Keep the mailbox clear of debris and overgrowing plants and ensure it is clearly numbered.

Child safety in the garden

● Make sure pool fences are maintained and gates closed when young children are about.

● Young children are fascinated with water, so they must be supervised at all times around ponds and pools; empty your wading pool when it is not in use, and never leave your child alone when in the water.

● Lock garages and sheds.

● Keep play areas well away from driveways.

● Keep play equipment in good condition.

● Children can fall from high play equipment or household furniture. Supervise, and provide a soft undersurfacing to any garden play equipment.

● Trim branches at children's eye level.

● Keep pathways clear.

● Ensure that your own garden has safe, secure fencing with self-latching gates.

BASIC GARDEN CLEANING EQUIPMENT

■ Wire brush	■ Bucket	■ Newspaper	■ Outdoor broom
■ Scrubbing brush	■ Hose	■ Sponges	■ Rags

▨ Repairing broken fence posts

The weakest part of a panel fence, and the most likely to succumb to rot, is where the fence posts come into contact with the soil. It is at this point that the fence will break during strong winds, causing it to list or fall over.

1 When fence spikes have been used, a broken post is easily unbolted and replaced, but where posts are concreted in, it is almost impossible to pull the broken stump out from the concrete footing. By far the easiest option is to cut off the post at ground level and use a repair spike.

2 Drive the spike between the remains of the rotten post and the concrete that surrounds it, so it provides a socket to hold the replacement post. (Always use treated pine that is recommended for use below ground level to avoid problems with timber posts rotting.)

Keeping the driveway clean

If you always park your car in the same spot and you're concerned about drips of grease and oil, place a shallow metal tray filled with sawdust or fine sand under the engine area. To remove oil stains, first blot any excess with something absorbent such as old newspaper or cat litter (work it in with a stiff broom), then blot again with a rag soaked in a grease solvent. Suitable solvents include methylated spirits and turpentine. You can also try a strong household bleach cleaner. Make up a high-strength solution according to the manufacturer's instructions, apply liberally on the stain, leave for 10 minutes, then wash away.

Maintaining paths and paving

If your paved surfaces have been laid properly, then they should require little maintenance, other than an occasional hosing down. Too much dirt can cause surfaces to become slippery. This is especially dangerous on natural stone lying in shaded areas that might also attract algae.

Usually brushing with an outdoor broom is enough to keep bricks and stone pavers looking good, especially as a little weathering improves their appearance. If mould and mildew become a problem, however, scrub the bricks and pavers with a mild solution of household bleach, leave for 48 hours, then rinse with a hose.

Removing weeds between pavers by digging, snipping or pulling out is kindest on the environment. You can also try killing them with hot water. Borax is a low-risk weed killer, but don't use it where it could leach onto beds or lawn as it is poisonous to all plants and doesn't discriminate.

Sweep concrete paths and pavers regularly with a stiff brush and occasionally wash them with hot water and detergent. To spruce up concrete, sprinkle cement powder over wet concrete and leave for about 10 minutes before sweeping up the excess.

Jet washes

A jet wash can work wonders bringing a surface almost back to its brand new condition, but it is not ideal for all paved areas. The jet is so powerful that any loose laid aggregates set between paving slabs will be sent flying. A jet wash will reveal if there are any poor-quality mortar joints, so if you do need to re-point then jet washing can present you with a quick method of removing any old and crumbling mortar.

Repointing broken paving slabs

1 Any broken paving slabs or bricks in your patio should be removed and replaced quickly to prevent anyone from tripping on them, resulting in possible injury. A slab or brick set into the middle of a terrace is far harder to replace than one on the edge of it and you will probably need to break it out using a club (lump) hammer and bolster.

2 Once the slab has been removed, chip out the old mortar bed.

3 Spread a depth of new mortar in its place and lower a new slab back into the correct position.

4 Finish the process off by tapping the slab down firmly. This can be done by using a maul or a club hammer that is hit against a block of wood placed on the slab. After the new slab has been put in, the surrounding joints can be re-pointed.

Sand-bedded paving bricks are very straightforward to replace, which is why this type of paving is often used in urban settings where access to utility services may occasionally be required. Bricks within areas of paving that have settled can be lifted out quite easily. You might need to break out the first brick to gain access to all the others, but after that the bricks can be removed quickly from the pattern as there is no mortar holding them together.

Once a sufficient area of bricks has been removed, dry sand can be placed and screeded out before compacting, re-sanding and screeding to the correct level. The bricks are then re-laid and tapped into place to provide a seamless repair.

Cleaning and maintaining brickwork

Bricks are best cleaned with a solution of hydrochloric acid and water, 1 part acid to 20 parts water. Always add the acid to the water so the acid will be less likely to splash you.

Crumbling mortar and broken bricks can be replaced, and cracks repaired, without damaging the rest of the wall.

Repointing and replacing bricks

One of the most common problems of brick walls is crumbling mortar. If you see deteriorating joints, you can replace the mortar to prevent major faults developing. Broken bricks are removed and replaced the same way.

1 Use a plugging chisel and a club (lump) hammer to remove any mortar that is loose or around broken bricks. Remove the bed joint first, then the top joint and then the two cross joints. Remove the brick.

2 Clean the cavity. Use a paint brush to dampen the bricks to prevent the mortar from drying out too quickly.

3 Mix up mortar to make a suitable colour and consistency. Replace the mortar on the bed joint first, then the cross joints and then apply mortar to the top of the brick. Replace the brick slowly, making sure the mortar does not fall off. Ensure any gaps in the mortar are filled. You can support the brick on a piece of plywood as you slide it in.

4 Rejoint the mortar, making sure that it is jointed the same as the existing joints.

Fixing cracks in brickwork

Cracks appear in brickwork when the structure settles or shifts. They should be repaired before they get too large.

1 Remove the mortar to a depth of at least 5 cm (2½ inches) or until the mortar is solid.

2 Then replace the mortar as described above. Cracks that reappear may indicate a serious problem. Consult a professional.

Painting exterior surfaces

Exterior surfaces need to be painted often because of the effect the environment has on them. Modern paint finishes respond well to weathering but still require occasional maintenance.

Preparing surfaces for painting

Basic cleaning down every 12 months, or a freshening up of heavy-duty areas, should provide a longer-lasting paint finish on exterior surfaces. Remember that dirt, grime and the sun are continually working away at the painted surface, breaking it down. Regular maintenance will make exterior repainting a much easier task, largely decreasing the amount of surface deterioration.

Modern homes require little maintenance, if any, apart from a regular washing down, while older homes, which generally have more timber surfaces, require much more work.

Tips for exterior painting

- Work from the top downwards, both when cleaning and painting, to prevent dust, dirt or paint splashes.

- Avoid painting in direct sunlight. Glare off the surface can hurt your eyes and put you at risk of skin cancer. Sunlight can cause many problems with the drying process and the ultimate paint finish. Try working on the shady side of the house in the morning, followed by the western, then the non-shady side, and finishing in the afternoon on the eastern side of the house.

- Complete all surface preparation before applying any paint or you will end up with damaged work. Keep to a system: surface preparation first, then priming, undercoat and finish.

- If the weather looks indifferent, consider painting areas that will not be damaged by wind and rain. Leave areas that are under cover until last, just in case it does rain.

HOMEMADE WINDOW CLEANERS

RECIPE 1	RECIPE 2	RECIPE 3
1 cup white vinegar	½ cup white vinegar	1 cup methylated spirits
4 litres (8½ pints) water	½ cup household ammonia	(denatured alcohol)
	4 litres (8½ pints) water	1 cup water

Cleaning windows

There is something very satisfying about seeing sun stream through a gleamingly clear pane of glass. Like any job, you need the best tools to do it properly.

You'll need the following equipment:

- Steady ladder to reach higher windows. Call a window cleaner if you're unsteady on your feet or suffer from vertigo.

- Bucket of cleaning solution — either a commercial one, or see the homemade alternatives above

- Sponge

- Squeegee — handle with a thin strip of sponge on one side and a rubber strip on the other

- Clean cloth

- Newspaper

Getting started

If you plan to clean or wash the window frames too, do these before you wash the glass. Wipe or dust the frames first and if that's not enough, follow with a wash and wipe dry. The best sort of day to wash windows is a cloudy one as sun on the windows causes the glass to dry too quickly and unevenly, resulting in streaks.

First, starting at the top of the window, wash the window with a cloth or sponge. Some people swear by rinsing with clean water then a wipe with a chamois, others not. It probably depends on how dirty the windows were to begin with and whether this is a grand annual ritual or a fortnightly routine. Following the wash or the rinse, squeegee the surface or dry it with a clean, dry, lint-free cloth.

For really dry, sparkly windows, polish with a few sheets of newspaper.

Window-cleaning tips

- To prevent windows from fogging, rub over a little glycerine after cleaning them.

- For a quick clean, when the glass is not too dirty: try wiping windows first with wet newspaper, then with dry. The ink on the newspaper gives them a polish.

- Never try to clean a window with a dry cloth as the dirt could scratch the glass.

- Never use soap on windows as it leaves smears that are very difficult to remove.

- To remove wet paint from glass, wipe with a cloth dipped in the appropriate solvent — turpentine for oil-based paints, water for water-based paint.

- To remove old paint marks from glass, gently scrape the paint with a razor blade, taking care not to scratch the glass.

- To remove putty marks from glass, wipe with ammonia or cold tea.

SHOO FLY!
Place fly-deterrent plants at doorways, on verandas and so on. These plants include lavender, sweet woodruff, lemon verbena, mint, thyme, rosemary, bay, chamomile and basil.

Flyscreens

First, remove dust and cobwebs from flyscreens with a soft brush, then wipe over with a sponge dipped in warm water. Rinse with clean water to which a few drops of citronella or tea-tree oil have been added.

Ventilators

Vents in your house walls need checking and cleaning so air can breeze through. Make sure you prune nearby trees and shrubs. Clean small holes with a bottle brush.

Keeping gutters clear

The only gutters worth having are clean ones: leaf- and dirt-filled ones don't work properly when it rains and are a fire hazard in dry, hot weather. To prevent a serious build-up of leaves and other debris, fit mesh along the gutter. This will protect the downpipes from blockage.

Clean gutters regularly. Use a trowel, plastic scraper or stiff brush to remove debris and built-up dirt, then give the gutters a good hose. Check the downpipe on a regular basis for blockages; use hot water to loosen any encrusted dirt before flushing the pipe with the hose.

Caring for garden furniture

- Furniture made from sealed wood should be wiped with a damp sponge dipped in a detergent solution. Keep an eye on cracks in the sealer and renew it regularly to maintain effective protection.

- Give unsealed wood a protective coat once a year by rubbing in a mixture of 4 parts raw linseed oil and 1 part turpentine.

- Wash cane furniture with warm, salty water and leave it to dry in the sun. Protect cane pieces by painting them with an outdoor lacquer.
- Wash canvas furniture as you would canvas awnings (see below).
- Lubricate metal hinges with oil or petroleum jelly.
- Use a chamois cloth to wipe over metal frames. Liquid wax polish helps prevent rusting.

Maintaining awnings and garden umbrellas

Brush off dirt and debris then scrub with a stiff-bristled brush dipped in warm water and detergent. Rinse. For stubborn stains, sprinkle with bicarbonate of soda, leave for 5 minutes, then rinse.

Remove mildew stains with a weak solution of bleach, but test for colour-fastness first. Leave the bleach solution for 48 hours, then rinse. Or, to avoid bleach, try rubbing the mildew with half a cut lemon dipped in salt. Always allow canvas to dry completely before putting it away.

FIRST AID FOR BEE AND WASP STINGS

Bees Remove the sting by scraping it sideways. This reduces the chance of more venom being released. Wipe the affected area clean. Apply a paste of bicarbonate of soda and water to the sting site. Wrap a bag of ice in a towel and hold it over the sting.

Wasps Daub the sting area with cider vinegar. Wrap a bag of ice in a towel and hold it over the sting.

Minimizing mosquitoes

- Eliminating the breeding sites is the key to reducing mosquitoes.
- Check the garden, daily if necessary, for small pools of water. Mosquitoes breed in the tiniest amounts of water, such as in plant saucers, paint cans, empty pots or plastic sheeting.

- Stock your pond with frogs and fish, which feed on mosquito larvae and help keep them under control.

- If you're in the garden after dusk, protect your skin by wearing long sleeves and long trousers.

- Flyscreens over open windows are the best way of keeping mosquitoes out of the house.

- Coils that burn allethrin repel mosquitoes to some degree.

- Citronella and lavender oils may be used as repellents.

The barbecue

A built-in barbecue can become a feature in your garden and an integral part of your outdoor lifestyle. It will, however, require time and money in construction, so be sure you will use it often enough to justify the work. In some cases a portable or mobile unit may suit your lifestyle better. Here are some points to consider when choosing a barbecue:

- For any barbecue you will need a level site and, preferably, one close to the house, but for a built-in barbecue it will have to be large enough for the structure and for the cook and helpers to move safely around it.

- The area where you entertain may not be suited to a built-in barbecue (it may be a deck or tiled patio) and so you may have to settle for a portable or mobile unit.

- You will need to have time and basic bricklaying or stone-working skills to build the barbecue, or be prepared to pay a professional to do the job.

- If you usually barbecue for only a couple of people, it may be a waste of fuel to use a large, built-in structure.

- Likewise, if you have many of your barbecues away from home (on picnics or holidays) you may find a portable barbecue more useful.

- You will probably find the cost of a built-in barbecue is similar to that of an equivalent mobile type.

Keeping the barbecue clean

The heat of a barbecue burns off old grease and dirt, but you can prevent the build-up of burnt remains in the first place by doing a little cleaning up after a cooking session. Brush off what you can with a wire brush, then wipe with scrunched up old newspaper. Give metal cooking plates an extra rub with a little salt or sand while they're still warm and oil them before storing.

Composting

By far the largest proportion of household rubbish consists of kitchen scraps, which are highly biodegradable and can be composted. As well as diverting rubbish away from landfill or garbage tips, composting provides you with valuable fertilizer for your garden. Alternatively, your local authority may know of community gardens that would welcome composting materials.

Constructing a compost heap

The secret to good composting is layering. Whether you create your own heap in a corner of your garden or use a special compost container from a gardening store, start with some basic layers, as follows.

1 Start off with a layer of woody prunings to raise the heap and allow air to circulate.

2 Next, add garden trimmings such as prunings and old plants, plus fruit and vegetable peel.

3 Add a third layer of grass cuttings and leaves.

4 Repeat these three layers to speed up the rotting process.

5 Finally, cover the heap with a piece of old carpet or straw to prevent moisture escaping and to keep heat within the compost heap.

As you add to the compost, intersperse moist and dry layers. Keep the heap damp but not wet to encourage the breakdown of material. Turn the heap regularly to improve aeration, which in turn speeds up the rotting process.

If your compost heap appears to be attracting cockroaches, maggots, rats or mice, add grass clippings to raise the internal temperature of the heap and keep pests at bay.

Composting checklist

Almost any biodegradable household waste can be composted:

- **Fruit and vegetable peelings** Some are particularly valuable. For instance, banana peel is high in potassium.
- **Tea and coffee** Tea leaves are rich in nitrogen. Coffee grounds contain protein and oils.
- **Waste paper** Cardboard and paper are useful because of their carbon content. Place cardboard at the bottom of the heap or packed around the sides. Paper works best if shredded.
- **Meat and fish** These are suitable for composting but they tend to attract flies and sometimes vermin. Place them directly in the inside of an already composting heap and the heat will be sufficient to break down the flesh and kill maggots, while a covering of soil and grass clippings or sawdust will deter flies.

Deodorizing garbage bins

Regularly washing your bins with detergent helps to keep the smells at bay. Scrub off hardened dirt with a stiff-bristled brush and rinse with the garden hose. To deter flies, wipe around the top of each bin with citronella or tea-tree oil. Alternatively, soak strips of old sheet in a repellent solution made from 10 drops citronella oil and 3 drops peppermint oil mixed in 1 litre (1¾ pints) water. Hang the strips inside the bin.

Collecting rainwater

Rainwater can be collected straight from the sky into bins and barrels for watering the garden or washing the car. But much more can be obtained by channelling it from the roof into a tank. If you are thinking of installing a rainwater tank, check with your local authority about restrictions on size, height and location of the tank. Depending on what you intend to use the water for, you'll also need to consider the capacity of the tank. The average household uses hundreds of litres or gallons of water a day; rainfall varies considerably from place to place.

Water from heaven

A sophisticated rainwater collecting system could work like this:

- Rain falls on the roof and enters covered guttering. Covered gutters keep out leaves and other solid matter that is on the roof.

- Water flows from the downpipe through another type of mesh that acts as a backstop to keep out any leaves which somehow entered the gutter.

- The first 10 or so litres (2½ gallons) of collected rain wash straight to the garden, and only after the roof has had a good clean is water diverted to another filtering device, called a sump, and then to the rainwater tank.

- A pump attached to the rainwater tank allows you to use water from the tank for household appliances such as washing machines and dishwashers that require a minimum water pressure in order to operate.

- Regular testing of the collected water indicates how suitable it is for drinking. Filters can also be fitted to taps to eliminate any lead in the water that may be present in the rainwater or leached from piping in the house.

WILDLIFE IN THE GARDEN

- To encourage birds, let a few plants go to seed, or install a birdbath, bird table or feeder in your garden.
- Ponds, and the plants around them, provide food and shelter for frogs, bees, dragonflies, birds and lizards.
- Rocky outcrops attract lizards.
- A small sunny spot is ideal for a patch of unmown grass that will attract butterflies and other insects.

The water meter

The first thing you should do when you move into a new house or unit is find the water meter and check it to make sure the washer works and actually shuts the water down. Quite often you go to a water meter in an emergency and it needs repairs and the water can't be shut down. If this is the case, putting a new washer in the meter is unfortunately a job for the plumber, but it will be money well spent. Otherwise, when the pipe bursts in the kitchen, and water goes everywhere, you will turn the water off at the main and nothing will happen.

The water main is usually on the left-hand side of the front garden, or if you live in an apartment it can actually be inside. Sometimes it's in the kitchen cabinet — just look for a tap under a cupboard that is on its own. Turn it off and test the water.

If there's a burst pipe in the house and you go to the meter, but it's not shutting the water down properly, look for a hose tap right next to the meter. Turn it on full, as well as any other tap between the meter and the burst pipe. This will reduce the flow in the house, not stop it, but it might save some damage until you can call a professional in.

Maintaining water features

Water features are a delightful addition to the garden, and don't require too much maintenance to keep them looking good. However, don't leave them unattended for long periods of time, or they will deteriorate.

Ponds

A healthy pond looks after itself: its ecosystem of plants and animals acts like a living filter. But if this system gets out of balance and the pond becomes choked with vegetation, or fish become diseased, you need to take action. Seek the advice of an aquarium expert before emptying the pond and possibly fitting a filter.

Swimming pools

You'll need plenty of equipment to keep your pool hygienic and clear of leaves and other debris. Chlorine or other chemicals keep bacteria and algae counts down. You can test for the right chlorine and pH levels with special kits. Scrub algae off the steps and pool sides with a nylon brush. Specialized vacuum cleaners and filter systems clean the water but you'll also need to regularly skim a leaf net over the surface.

Keeping the area around the pool tidy and free of leaves will help keep the pool clean too. Sweep regularly and keep plants trimmed, and make sure pavers are free of mould by cleaning them regularly with a mild solution of bleach. Leave for 48 hours, then rinse and brush with a stiff outdoor brush.

Spas

Regularly empty and clean your outdoor spa by following the manufacturer's instructions. If you plan to keep the spa constantly full, you'll need a filter system.

Water features and child safety

Water seems to have a magnetic quality for children so safety is extremely important. There are some points to remember if the two are definitely going to meet.

Choose water features that can be covered with a grid and a layer of cobbles, such as wall fountains, springs and cascades. If you decide to construct a raised pool, then build the walls at least 60 cm (2 ft) high and overhang coping stones.

If you really want an open water feature, make sure that the garden you create has a separated area with child-proof locks. As an extra precaution use a grid just under the water's surface, strong enough to support a child's weight. Also, make pool edges as safe as possible with heavy marginal planting, and ensure that the paving is not mossy and slippery.

The garden shed

All too often the garden shed or garage becomes a dumping ground where all the nasty stuff you don't want to keep in the house gets stored: solvents, paints, weed killers, insecticides and sharp, heavy tools. The chemicals are potentially hazardous when inhaled or ingested, or when they come into contact with the skin; they are also a major cause of accidental poisoning, particularly among young children.

A tidy shed is not only more efficient — it is obviously much safer as well. Also, you may well want to use your garden shed as a work area, so it's vital that the space is safe to inhabit for a few hours.

Commonsense storage

- If you have children, the best protection is a good lock on the shed door.
- Never store flammable substances near heating devices or open flames.
- Take care that pressurized containers are not punctured or subjected to undue pressure (don't put a heavy tool box on top of them).
- Never store petrol in plastic containers.
- Never store dangerous chemicals in empty soft drink bottles or food containers. It is best to keep poisonous substances in their original containers.
- Contact your local poisons information service about the safe disposal of chemicals you no longer require. Under no circumstances should you put them down the drain.

Terrific tools

- Keeping your tools clean and sharp makes them safer to use and extends their life.
- Clean tools by wiping them with a damp cloth or, if necessary, washing them in a detergent solution. Dry them with a clean, dry rag and hang them up if possible.
- Disinfect pruning saws and secateurs after use to prevent the spread of fungal diseases.
- Keep a can of rough grease or oil with a rag in it and rub it over the metal parts of tools to prevent rusting.

- Wipe over the wooden handles of tools with linseed oil every few months.
- Sharpen the backs of cutting edges by rubbing them on a sandstone or an oilstone every year.

Organizing a work area

If you are planning on having a work area in your garden shed, cross-ventilation is ideal to counteract any fumes. If possible, locate your work space between a door and a window. Consider fan-assisted ventilation if you are unable to get a good cross-flow of air.

Windows can supply enough daylight to work by. If a window is not available, skylights are excellent alternatives and simple to install. If you need artificial lighting, 150-watt halogen floodlights are preferable to fluorescent lighting, which distorts colours and gives rise to a phenomenon where a rotating part spinning fast appears to be stationary. This is a safety hazard when you are using variable speed machines, such as routers, drills and lathes.

You will require a sturdy, flat work surface, such as a wooden bench or table, and sufficient space to assemble and manoeuvre your projects. If your work space will be shared with other activities, consider a folding workbench and lockable shadow board for tool storage. In a small space, a wall-mounted bench or a bench with storage underneath will be more useful. If you are lucky enough to have a large, dedicated workshop, a freestanding workbench will give you the greatest flexibility.

If you have any fixed machinery, such as a table saw, drill press or lathe, try to arrange it so that movement between the various work stations with your projects is easy and relaxed.

The floor surface should be easy to sweep and keep clean. Cover or eliminate spaces under cupboards and shelves, where dust and dropped items can be difficult to recover.

Pendant, general-purpose electrical outlets are convenient and safe. Hanging above the work area, they keep the cords of portable tools away from the workbench or floor where they might accidentally be damaged or tripped over, as well as providing a greater working range for the tools.

inside

In an ideal world we would all like an organized house that is clutter-free, healthy and safe for the whole family as well as any pets. This chapter comes to the rescue and provides invaluable hints on one of the hardest household jobs — throwing things away that you no longer need — as well as information on dealing with household allergies, running an environmentally friendly house, home safety and living with pets.

Clutter control

Clutter makes it harder to clean and harder to find things when you want them. Whether it's piles of paper hiding the dining room table, dozens of empty jars that you think you might need one day, or stashes of pens that don't work, clutter of one sort or another is very often the root of a feeling of mildly unnerving chaos in the home. If you feel like this you most certainly are not alone. There are even people who earn a living by helping people declutter their lives — either as a personal service or in a workshop. A few time-tested principles may help you gradually clear your home and regain a sense of control.

Getting organized: The box method

Take six boxes or containers and sort your junk and treasures:

BOX 1: Throw away.

BOX 2: Give away or sell. Charity shops (thrift stores) need goods for raising money. Yard sales (or garage sales) and classified ads are ways you can sell it yourself.

BOX 3: Put away. Things to put away later, sorted by room if that's easy enough to do quickly.

BOX 4: Storage. This box is for seasonal clothing and items you only use occasionally such as camping equipment, decorating tools and archive documents.

BOX 5: Limbo (or the '1 year box'). This is the 'not sure' box where anything you're not sure about goes. It gets packed away for 1 year and if you never use it within that time, it's time to throw it out.

BOX 6: Needs repairs. Be realistic — will you actually fix it? Otherwise, it's into Box 1.

When it's overwhelming

When you feel as if you are never going to make progress:

Use the timer. Give yourself 5/10/30 minutes to tidy a room.

Count. Put away a set number of items — say, five or ten.

Start small. Go through one drawer or one shelf per session.

Get ruthless. Dump everything on the floor, then take back what you want to keep. To stay, an item needs to pass the clutter test:

- Is it in good shape?
- If it's broken, can it be fixed?
- Do you really need it?
- Have you used it in the past year?
- Would it be hard to replace if you ever need it again?
- Would you pay money to store it?
- Does it have sentimental value?

The paper chase

We have not achieved the paper-free home any more than the paperless office. Letters from school, invitations, newspaper clippings, bills, junk mail… There are times when you need a radical paper sort.

1 Put all your papers into a box. As you go, bin the items you don't need.

2 Sort the papers into the following categories. They may need halfway houses, such as boxes, till you find them more permanent homes:

- **Act on** Have a special spot for things you need to act on, such as bills — perhaps a special noticeboard or a folder that you go through regularly.
- **Personal** This is where letters, anniversary cards etc. are kept.
- **Banking** Statements, letters from the bank, spare cheque book.
- **House maintenance** The instructions for the air-conditioning or water heater, guarantees for appliances.
- **Expenses** Your dockets and invoices.
- **Tax** Anything that will be relevant when tax time comes around.
- **School** Sports dates, school calendars, permission notes, timetables.
- Finally, create an 'in' box which you empty and file once a week.

Staying uncluttered

- Spend 10 minutes each morning or evening picking things up and putting them back where they belong.
- Institute family or household rules for clearing up after one activity and before starting another.
- Deal with things as they arise.

Clutter control

The golden rule of clutter control: when in doubt, throw it out:

- Clothes that don't fit.
- Gifts you don't like and never intend using.
- Broken things you don't miss and are unlikely to ever get round to mending.
- Books you don't value.
- Appliances you never use.

Do it now!

- Take things upstairs when you're going anyway.
- Take things downstairs when you're going anyway.
- Pick up things when they drop.
- Wipe spills when they happen.
- Vacuum messes when they occur.
- File bills and correspondence immediately.
- Dump junk mail the minute you receive it.

Set limits

- Allow yourself a set number of bags, food containers and boxes that you keep because they 'might come in handy one day'.
- Pare down on mementoes. When the cupboards are bursting, clear and sort them, fill them in an orderly fashion, and find another

home for the excess, whether it's the garbage bin, shed, school fete or next garage sale.

- One in, one out. In other words, throw/give away one item each time you acquire another. This may be worth trying if you are constantly acquiring new things, be it from friends, charity shops (thrift stores) or car boot sales.

Allergy and the healthy house

Allergies can cause a range of symptoms from the irritating — such as a runny nose or a mild rash — to the life threatening, such as a severe asthma attack or anaphylactic shock. Living with an allergy such as hay fever or asthma is an unfortunate reality for many children and adults. What's more, the incidence of these problems is rising sharply — in some places the incidence of asthma has doubled over two decades — and doctors cannot say why.

While some allergies, such as hay fever, tend to be more severe outside the house, home sweet home can also harbour allergy triggers, or allergens. The main triggers around the house are dust mites, moulds, pollen spores and particles of skin and saliva from pets. These are all capable of triggering a range of allergy symptoms, especially ones involving the respiratory tract. All these triggers can also be found in household dust — hence an emphasis on tackling dust in the home.

Air cleaners

Several products — including ion generators, ozone generators, mechanical air filters, electronic air cleaners and hybrid air cleaners (which combine techniques) — are marketed as air cleaners. Ion generators act by charging particles in a room so they are attracted to surfaces such as walls and tabletops. Rubbing these surfaces can cause the particles to be re-suspended in the air. They may remove small particles such as those in tobacco smoke but cannot remove gases or odours, nor are they effective in removing larger particles such as pollen. Ion generators indirectly generate ozone, which is itself a lung irritant.

Improve your ventilation

- There are several measures you can take to improve the ventilation in your home.

- Fit extractors, also called exhaust fans, in the bathroom and kitchen. Exhaust fans need to be discharged to the outside air and not to an enclosed garage where they can cause problems of condensation, mould and rot. They are useful in wet rooms such as bathrooms as well as in garages and workshops where they can remove fumes.

- Install an overrun timer on the extractor fan in very steamy bathrooms.

- Fit air grilles, also known as trickle ventilators, into the window frames of living rooms and bedrooms.

- Maintain air-conditioning systems, especially filters.

Dust mites

House dust mites love warmth, humidity and, as their name suggests, dust. They are often microscopic in size, but they cause havoc to people who are allergic to their droppings. The term 'house dust mite' applies to about ten species of the Pyroglyphidae family of the arachnids. They thrive at a temperature of about 25°C (77°F) and relative humidity of 75 to 80 per cent, eating the skin flakes that humans shed constantly. Just like humans, house dust mites love soft furnishings — mattresses, pillows, soft carpets and upholstered furniture. They proliferate in conditions of humidity and poor ventilation, so good ventilation and moisture-reducing practices, such as fans in the bathroom and kitchen, help keep populations down. See 'The bedroom', page 233, for more practical tips on dealing with dust mites.

MIGHTY NUMBERS OF MITES
A double bed mattress can support a population of up to 2 million house dust mites. Under the right conditions a new mattress's mite population can reach this figure in just 3 months.

War on dust

If family members suffer dust-related allergies, there are a number of dust traps to avoid:

- Padded headboards, especially buttoned ones.
- Clutter and ornaments, unless they are behind glass.
- Books on open shelves.
- Heavy curtains. (Blinds, including roller blinds, are a better option, and vertical Venetian blinds collect less dust than horizontal ones.)
- Forced heating systems. (Vent coverings can help trap dust and prevent it from circulating in the house.)
- Carpets. (Tightly woven short-pile carpets are less dusty than long, loose weaves, but hard flooring, such as timber or tile, is even better.)
- Cracks between floorboards. (Seal cracks to prevent dust blowing up from the space beneath.)
- Evening cleaning in the bedroom. (Clean earlier in the day, as cleaning can stir up dust in the air that takes a while to settle.)

Mould

There are more mould spores in the air than any other biological particle: record counts are as high as 160,000 spores for every cubic metre (35 cubic feet) of air, compared to record counts of 2800 pollen particles per cubic metre (35 cubic feet). Reducing dampness is the first line of defence against moulds. Even simple measures such as wiping away condensation and opening up windows can help. In addition, look out for mould growth sites, such as old food and pot plants.

Pollen

People allergic to pollen need to be extra careful about what they let into the house, be it through an open window or on the soles of their shoes. People with severe pet allergies may decide not to own a pet at all, while others may find that as long as they are scrupulous about vacuuming, or they do not let a pet sleep on the bed, their symptoms are manageable.

Out-gases

A growing body of opinion classes reactions to the fumes from paints, fuel and furnishings as allergies. There is also the suggestion that excessive exposure to these fumes (which includes out-gasing) could make individuals more sensitive and more likely to develop classical allergic reactions. It is a controversial field, but as a general rule, water-based paints, stains and adhesives give off fewer odours and out-gases than solvent-based finishes. Smooth wall finishes offer fewer niches for allergens.

Defeating damp

A damp house is not a healthy one: it's all too easy for moulds and other fungus, bacteria and mites to proliferate. Fixing dampness first requires identifying the source of the problem:

- Rising damp is water rising from the ground. It is usually prevented by a damp course which may need fixing or replacing after a number of years.

- Penetrating damp occurs when water comes through a wall after heavy rain, possibly because of a leaking downpipe or gutter, or an entry point above the damp course.

- Condensation forms when water condenses from humid air and settles on cold surfaces such as windows or cold spots in poorly heated and badly ventilated rooms.

To reduce dampness:

- Check damp courses. In old houses they may be non-existent or disintegrated to the point where they are useless.

- Check downpipes, gutters and window surrounds. Rust or blockages might be causing water to flood or leak into vulnerable areas.

- Wipe condensation away from windows.

- Ventilate bathrooms and kitchens.

- Improve insulation. This helps to eliminate cold spots which, in turn, reduces condensation and associated mould growth.

The 'green' house

A green house is also a healthy house. When you decide to make your house 'greener', you are making a decision that affects not only your own household but the wider environment as well. 'Going green' means making your home as energy efficient as possible; treating all resources as precious rather than something to be thoughtlessly squandered; and in lots of small but important ways, reducing your impact on a fragile planet.

Many of the principles of an ecologically sound house also make economical sense. A house that has been designed to be energy efficient should be a naturally comfortable one too. Building a house from scratch allows you to situate, orient and shelter the building to make the best of renewable sources of energy. Ideally, living spaces should face north in the southern hemisphere (and south in the northern hemisphere) to take greatest advantage of the sun for light and warmth in both summer and winter. If you are renovating or extending an existing house, consult an environmental architect to discuss options for low-energy designs.

Energy-saving tips

Even if you are not planning to build a house, consider a few energy-efficient principles:

- Use the sun and wind where possible for energy, relying less on supplementary, non-renewable energy. This can be as simple as pegging out the washing rather than using your dryer — sun and wind are free.

- Think of the local environment: plant native trees and flowers, compost organic wastes, garden organically and use natural pest control. Use low-flush or waterless toilets, and collect, store and use rainwater.

- Use green materials and products. The green ideal is to use non-toxic, non-polluting products from sustainable and renewable sources, produced with low energy and low environmental and social costs, which are biodegradable or easily reused and recycled.

- Paint the exterior of a house with light-coloured paint to help reflect unwanted radiant heat.

- Shade all windows when it's warm or hot. Windows are a main entry point for heat and light — highly desirable in winter, but potentially overheating in summer. Consider ways of shading windows in the summertime — for example, with awnings and deciduous trees.

- Create a healthy indoor climate by allowing the house to breathe. Use natural materials and processes to regulate the temperature, humidity and air flow.

- If you live in a hot climate, open up and ventilate the house at night when the air is cooler.

- Allow sunlight and daylight to penetrate your home, and rely less on artificial lighting.

Solar energy

Sun-powered electricity, harnessed by solar panels on the roof, can run all your house's appliances and heat water for the bathroom and kitchen. In a solar hot water heater, the sun directly heats up water in small pipes, which is stored in a tank for later use, usually in conjunction with a gas or electrical heater to boost the temperature of the water. Photovoltaic cells on the roof convert the sun's energy to electricity, which can be diverted to the fridge, sound system and washing machine. In some systems surplus electricity is sent to the main electricity grid.

Every little bit counts

You'll be surprised at how quickly even small savings turn into big ones — for both you and the environment.

- Install a solar or energy-efficient hot water heater. Since water heating accounts for up to 50 per cent of a home's energy use, installing one of these solar heaters saves in energy bills as well as pollution.

- Choose energy-efficient appliances when buying new ones. Many countries have star ratings to make the choice easier. Top-rated fridges, freezers, washing machines, dryers, dishwashers and air-conditioners are much less polluting and also cheaper to run.

- Install a water-efficient showerhead. These usually pay for themselves in the first year of use. The shower is the largest user of household hot water and accounts for around 20 per cent of the greenhouse pollution in the average home. These showerheads use less water, reducing both pollution and heating costs.

- Insulate your home. Save on heating and cooling bills as well as the pollution these processes produce.

- Consider ways of adding thermal mass to your home if you live in a climate with cool winters. Thermal mass describes heavy building materials such as brick, stone or thick ceramic tiles that are slow to heat and slow to cool. In the winter they warm up in the day and continue to radiate heat in the evening, while in summer they protect against excessive heat, especially when shaded. New brick, tile or concrete flooring is an obvious way of adapting an existing home to include greater thermal mass.

- Use appliances only when you really need them. For instance, use a broom in the garden, not a motorized leaf blower.

- Use all your appliances efficiently and maintain them well so they work optimally.

- Defrost your freezer every 3 months to prolong its life and ensure maximum efficiency.

- Don't leave the fridge door open unnecessarily. For every minute it is open, it takes 3 minutes to cool down again.

- Always turn off your fridge and leave the door ajar when you go on holiday.

- Switch off lights when they are not in use.

- Replace your most frequently used light bulbs with compact fluorescents: each bulb uses around a quarter of the electricity needed for a standard bulb and will prevent the emission of half a tonne or ton of greenhouse pollution over the life of the bulb. If you fitted all your lamps and lights with energy-efficient bulbs, you could reduce your lighting costs by 80 per cent.

- Turn off microwaves, TVs and sound systems at the power point — they use power even when they are not operating.

- Wash clothes in cold water if you're satisfied with the result. Consider pre-soaking heavily soiled garments first.

- Wear adequate clothing when the weather is cool and don't attempt to heat the entire house to the same temperature. You should keep one or two rooms cosy by shutting the doors to the rest of the house.

Weather-proofing

Weather-proofing the house helps keep out cold draughts and rain. Consider taking the following measures:

- Apply weather strips to external doors.

- Seal gaps under skirting boards, around the edge of window frames and under windowsills.

- Check the ceiling for gaps where pipes leave roof spaces.

- Fill the cavity of outside walls with insulation in order to stop unwanted air leakage.

Water-wise tips

According to the World Health Organisation (WHO), the absolute minimum amount of water a person needs every day is 5.6 litres (1.5 gallons). In 1970 the WHO surveyed 91 countries and found an average water use of 22.7 litres (6 gallons) per head per day for people who used a public hydrant. In most countries consumption was below 45.4 litres (12 gallons) per head per day, but in the United States it was 272.5 litres (72 gallons) per head per day.

Water supplies the world over are strained to produce enough clean water to meet population demands without drying up reserves. Conserving water not only takes the strain off your local supplier but also reduces pollution, as water processing requires energy, which in turn creates pollution. Saving water can also save you money as, increasingly, local suppliers are charging for the amount of water a household uses.

Hot issues

Heating water burns up money as well as produces pollution. Try these simple ideas for reducing your hot water usage:

- Take quicker showers. Cutting your shower time from 10 minutes to 5 could save as much as 27,000 litres (5939 gallons) of water a year.

- Fix dripping taps. Forty-five drops of water a minute is 10 baths of water a year.

- Don't rinse dishes under a running hot tap. Use a sink or bowl full of water instead.

- Avoid turning the hot tap on for small quantities of water. This leaves the pipes full of hot water, which cools and is wasted.

- Turn off the hot water system if you'll be away from home for more than 2 or 3 days.

- Insulate your storage tank. Between 15 and 20 per cent of the cost of running an electric hot water service is due to heat losses from the storage tank. Reduce losses by wrapping the tank in foil-backed insulating blanket held in place with ducting tape. (Do not add extra insulation to gas systems as they may overheat.)

- Install solar hot water heaters if possible when making big changes on your house.

- Install an on-demand system if you have a choice, as they are the most efficient — you are not paying to heat stored water.

- Locate new hot water systems near where you use hot water to cut the amount of hot water and energy lost through cooling in pipes.

TOILET TRICKS
Up to one-third of water used in the home is flushed down the toilet. Save water by fitting a dual flush to your toilet cistern. Consider, too, ways to reuse bath/handbasin water. See page 212.

Safe and sound

A few general safety principles will go a long way towards making your home a safer one to live in, especially if you have children.

Electricity

Adults sustain most electrical injuries during DIY activities, while children are more at risk from 'mending' electrical equipment and pushing objects into sockets. Safety switches, or circuit breakers, can save lives and prevent injuries by turning off the electricity when they detect current passing out of the circuit. To minimize risks, keep the following in mind:

- If using electrically operated power tools, invest in a special 'cut off' device. In the event of the cable being accidentally cut, the device will shut down the electricity supply to the tool. This piece of equipment is commonly called a residual current circuit device or earth leakage device.

- Keep wiring and appliances in good order and do not use them if you suspect they are faulty.

WHAT TO DO IF THE POWER GOES OUT

It depends on what you've got in your meter box. You may have the more old-fashioned ceramic fuses or the new breakers.

Fuses

1 Turn off the main switch. Take out the ceramic fuse and check to see if the wire running through it is broken. If it is, the fuse has blown.

2 Simply undo the screws enough to remove the wire and replace it with the same size. The amp size of the wire is written on the fuse — for example, 20A, 8A.

Breakers

1 Put it back and turn the main on. If the fuse blows again, it's best to get an electrician in.

2 If you have the new system, with breakers, it's simple. All your switches should be ON. When you open the meter box, simply look for the breaker that has tripped to OFF. Just turn it on. If it trips again to OFF, you should call an electrician.

- Keep all electrical appliances out of reach of children.

- Consider fitting power point covers.

- Never use electrical appliances in wet areas.

- Always remember to turn off the power before removing a plug from a power point.

- Do not attempt electrical repairs if you are not qualified.

Ladder safety

Ladders and steps are invaluable for gaining access to higher levels. Although simple tools they are often abused and can lead to nasty accidents if used incorrectly. By obeying the following rules you will minimize the risk of injury:

- The distance from the base of the wall or skirting board to the foot of the ladder must be a quarter of the height the ladder rests at.

- The base of the ladder must rest on a level, non-slip surface.

- Both foot pads must touch the ground — you may shim with plywood pads but keep the ladder level.

- Ensure that the top of the ladder always has total contact with the wall surface.

- Before mounting a ladder, check all rungs are secure and have not been damaged in any way.

- If using a ladder outdoors watch out for overhead powerlines and telephone cables.

- Never overstretch — if you cannot reach comfortably, you should move the ladder.

- When working at any height have a helper hold the bottom of the ladder to prevent it moving.

Lifting

The timber used in floors and stairways can be very heavy and unwieldy, so ask someone to help when lifting boards and joists. Do not lift more than you can safely carry — it is better to make an extra journey and take longer to finish the job than to risk injury by carrying too much. When lifting, bend your knees, not just your waist. Wear gloves to protect your hands from rough concrete and timber splinters.

Drilling

Never drill into an area of a wall, floor or ceiling where there is likely to be electric cables or gas and water pipes behind. Use a joist, pipe and cable detector to locate the exact position of such services before starting work. Read the operating instructions carefully to ensure that you are using the detector accurately.

Before the widespread introduction of power tools, there was a plethora of attachments for electric drills that did everything from sawing to sanding. These are both less efficient and less safe than stand-alone power tools.

Smoke alarms

Smoke alarms give an early warning of fire, the chance to escape and an earlier opportunity to call the fire brigade. They are inexpensive and very easy to install. One, preferably two, smoke alarms per household is the minimum recommended by fire safety experts. Research shows that 10 to 15 per cent of smoke alarms in homes don't work properly, so it's important to change the battery regularly and check monthly that smoke alarms are working.

Toxic materials

Some older properties may contain asbestos products or insulation. If you come across suspected asbestos get it removed by a specialist contractor.

Lead was added to paint until fairly recently and can be released into the atmosphere if an old finish is burnt off. Remove lead-based paints with paint stripper before recoating, rather than with a blow-lamp or hot air gun. Modern paints and varnishes are far less toxic but they should still be handled with care. Read the instructions on the can carefully and apply them at all times, particularly regarding brush cleaning and disposal of excess paint. Remove paint from skin with a proprietary hand cleaner not white spirit, which strips essential oils from the skin and can lead to dermatitis in extreme cases.

Avoid breathing the heavy vapour from adhesives. Pay attention to any warning on the can and make sure you always work in a well-ventilated space whenever possible. If you start to feel light headed, stop work immediately and go outside into the fresh air.

Out of reach

Keep all dangerous items such as matches, knives, kettles and their cords out of reach of young children. Keep all cleaners and other chemicals either high up or in a locked cupboard. Store medicines well out of reach.

Prevent scalds

Hot water burns like fire. The main risks are from hot drinks, kettles and saucepans being knocked over or pulled down and from tap water. Reducing the temperature of your hot water to 50°C (122°F) greatly lowers the risk of scalds: it takes only 1 second for a major burn at 60°C (140°F), 10 seconds at 55°C (131°F), yet 5 minutes at 50°C (122°F). If it's impossible to alter the temperature of your hot water, consider installing mixing valves or other devices that limit the temperature of water at the tap. See also page 151.

Prevent falls

Consider areas where babies and toddlers could fall. Install stair gates top and bottom, and closely examine balcony areas for safety. Effective gates and barriers are ones that can't be climbed. Elderly or infirm family members can fall in slippery bathrooms. If appropriate, install non-slip flooring and safety rails in your bathroom.

Fire exits

Make sure you have an alternative route of escape in the case of fire and keep it clear of obstacles. If your windows are barred, make sure that at least one can be opened with a key. If you dead-lock your doors at night, keep the key by your bedside.

A rehearsed fire exit plan can really help children survive a fire as they are at high risk of smoke inhalation and asphyxiation. Use phrases like 'Stop, drop and roll' and 'Get down low and go go go' to help them remember the fire drill.

Entranceway lighting

Lamps that light up driveways, paths and front doors help young and old alike to avoid falls, and deter intruders from lurking in the shadows.

Child safety around the home

Parents are always worried about harm coming to their child, but one of the biggest threats to child safety can actually be the home. Here are some useful child-proofing tips. (See also page 148.)

- When babies and toddlers are on the move, they will be dipping into everything, so constant supervision is vital. Even when your child is asleep, check on him, and always make sure no items that could choke or suffocate him are within reach.

- Reinforce warnings — such as 'that's hot', 'don't touch', 'take care' and 'ouch' — so children gain an understanding of words and phrases that teach caution.

- Place safety latches on all the drawers and cupboards that contain potentially harmful products such as dishwashing powder and plastic bags, or implements such as knives, skewers, toothpicks and any object that could cause choking. Always reserve a special cupboard or drawer for your child and fill it with items that can be used as musical instruments, for shop games or measuring and pouring fun.

- Avoid sharp edges and corners on furniture that can injure.

- Avoid toy boxes with heavy lids. Use baskets in the rooms where your child plays.

- Cover electrical outlets with safety caps.

- Place electrical cords out of reach: run them along the wall or behind furniture.

- Check that your child's collection of toys is child-safe (see the box on page 45).

- Many children are injured by furniture falling on top of them as they hold onto it to pull themselves up, or try to climb on it.

Bookshelves and wardrobes can be particularly dangerous. If furniture is in danger of tipping over, it's a good idea to bolt it to the wall. Push appliances to the back of shelves or tables, away from the edge.

● Don't leave tiny objects lying around on the floor, such as coins, marbles or beads, that a small child could pick up and choke on.

● Never leave a nappy bucket on the floor or in a place where your child could fall into it.

● Place safety gates at the top and bottom of stairs, and be careful to check that a toddler is not able to climb over them.

TOY SAFETY CHECKLIST

Before you give your child a toy to play with, run through this safety checklist first.

■ Is it safe?

■ Is it age appropriate? Check the label.

■ Is it unbreakable?

■ Is it washable?

■ Is it too big to swallow?

■ Does it have any sharp edges or other pointy bits?

■ Does it have any strings, cords or ribbons that are longer than 15 cm (6 inches) attached?

■ Is it made from non-toxic materials?

■ Does it run on batteries or electricity? (Batteries are dangerous if children suck them.)

■ Does it have any small gaps that can pinch fingers?

■ Does it make any loud explosive sounds that could damage a baby's hearing?

■ Avoid toys that are smaller than a roll of film canister as they are potential choking hazards.

In an emergency

A little forethought saves time and hassle later. Stick a list of emergency phone numbers somewhere prominent so that all members of the household can find them easily if they need them. Make sure the medicine cabinet and first aid kit are well stocked at all times.

Emergency phone nos:

- Family doctor
- Nearest hospital with accident and emergency unit
- Local police station
- Local fire station
- Plumber
- Locksmith
- Glazier
- Electrician
- Electricity company's emergency phone number
- Local gas emergency number
- Local builder
- Vet
- Work numbers of the adults in the household
- School/day care numbers (as appropriate)
- Relatives or friends whom children can ring in an emergency

Living with pets

Medical studies demonstrate that pets help to keep us healthy as they have a comforting and calming effect. They can, however, create more dirt, and if a member of your household suffers from allergies, you may need to take extra care looking after a pet and its belongings. Ensuring good ventilation and cleaning regularly can minimize the effect of pet allergens; keeping pets out of bedrooms and off beds will also help to reduce exposure to allergens.

Common pet allergies

While you can, in theory, be allergic to any animal, there are some pets that are more likely to cause problems.

- **Cats** These animals are known for their meticulous grooming, which usually consists of much licking from head to tail. When the saliva dries, it flakes and floats off, landing on surfaces around the home. It is this dried saliva that contains the allergen protein which can trigger allergy symptoms such as asthma and a runny nose in sufferers. The particles are so light and small they spread easily, and even a tiny amount can be enough to cause problems. Cat saliva flakes are also highly persistent and unless a place is washed thoroughly after a cat leaves, they can remain for years.

- **Dogs** Allergens are present in dog's saliva and skin particles. These may be carried by fur, but the hairs themselves do not trigger allergic reactions.

- **Mice** The urine of small creatures such as mice and hamsters is a common allergic trigger.

Pet etiquette

Minimize the transfer of bacteria and other disease-causing organisms from pets to humans.

- Wash your hands after handling a pet, especially before eating.

- Keep cats and other mobile pets off food preparation surfaces.

- Give pets their own plates and bowls — do not share family ones with pets — and wash them every day.

- Do not encourage begging at the table.

Keeping pets clean and odour-free

Homes with pets often smell of the pets themselves. Regular attention will minimize odours and keep the pets themselves comfortable and free of fleas and lice.

- Cages, perches, baskets and toys need regular cleaning in hot, soapy water. A salty rinse and drying in the sun disinfects without leaving harmful residues.

- All bedding should be washed frequently and dried in the sun.

- Pets themselves also need regular grooming and bathing.

- Allow pets outside for some of the day, if possible.

- Regularly remove droppings from litter trays — more than daily if necessary. Place the tray in an area of good ventilation.

- Don't leave litter trays near where food is prepared or eaten.

- Wash litter boxes frequently in hot sudsy water.

- Frequently vacuum any areas in the house used by pets.

- Increase the frequency of shampooing of carpets and upholstery.

- Use bicarbonate of soda between shampoos on carpets and upholstery: sprinkle generously, leave for 15 minutes then vacuum.

On the nose

- The smell of pet urine on concrete is difficult to remove. To deodorize it, scrub the surface with a solution of half white vinegar and half water, or spray with methylated spirits (denatured alcohol).

- To deodorize a smelly litter tray, wash it in hot, soapy water, rinse in salt water then white vinegar and hot water, and dry in the sun.

Bathing a pet

- Use a non-slip mat in a tub to ease fears of slipping.

- Cover the drain with an inverted tea strainer to prevent hairs sliding down the drain and blocking the pipes.

Banish fleas

There are many species of flea, but the main ones to worry about in the home are the ones that prefer humans, cats and dogs (*Siphonaptera*). If you have a cat or a dog, tackling its flea infestation — or even better, making sure one doesn't happen in the first place — is the priority.

- Vacuuming is the number one defence against fleas. As well as removing the fleas themselves, it also removes eggs and larvae. But vacuuming fleas does not kill them, so you'll need to replace the vacuum bag after each session (and seal the full bag in a plastic bag and leave it in the sun to kill the fleas, before disposing of it). If you have a non-disposable bag, place a little pyrethrin insecticide inside the bag before you begin.

- Wash your pet weekly. Use shampoos with essential oils such as pennyroyal, eucalyptus and tea-tree or add 1 drop of lemongrass or citronella oil to your pet's regular shampoo. If you're considering mainstream shampoos, malathion is the least toxic. Others may contain methoprene and pyrethroid products such as permethrin.

- Wash your pet's bedding frequently in hot soapy water. In a high infestation period such as midsummer it's a good idea to do this at least weekly.

- To repel fleas and deodorize, wipe over pet belongings with water to which a few drops of tea-tree oil have been added. Use it also as a final rinse for a kennel floor and litter trays. (Do not use it undiluted as it is poisonous when concentrated.)

- Comb your pet with a flea comb.

- Consider steam-cleaning rugs and upholstery seasonally.

- For a bad infestation, use a pyrethrin treatment in cracks, crevices, carpets and your pet's bedding or sleeping places. This paralyses the fleas, allowing them to be vacuumed up.

- Flea powders containing dust of rotenone and pyrethrins are not highly toxic but do not last long and need to be reapplied often.

- As a last resort, use a permethrin/methropene flea bomb. The former chemical kills adult fleas while the latter stops new hatchlings reaching maturity.

- Your vet may recommend monthly skin treatments and quarterly injections which also break the flea life cycle. It may be necessary to use other control methods too, however, as these only take effect once a flea has bitten its host.

living area

The living area of your home — which usually centres around the lounge room or family room — is where you relax, socialize and probably watch television. It is also a place where you may entertain guests, so it is a busy area, as well as one that is often on display, so it needs to be a place of comfort as well as order and beauty. Whether you need tips on caring for floors, doors, walls, ceilings, windows, furniture or your electrical equipment, this chapter is packed with indispensable advice.

The ideal living room

The clever living room is multifunctional and comfortable for the whole household. It is easy to care for and, with adequate storage, clutter-free.

- During the day the room is a bright and enjoyable place to be, lit by natural light.

- In the summer, the room is appealing because it is cool and fresh and in the winter, a comforting place into which you can retreat, leaving the cold and dark outside.

- Quarry tiles on a thick concrete base act as a solar heat store, remaining cool in the summer and warm in the winter. This minimizes dust and dust mites, and is easy to clean.

- The walls are painted with washable satin-finish, water-based paint.

- Woollen rugs add extra warmth underfoot.

- Double-glazed windows reduce outside noise and help regulate the temperature, while window vents provide ventilation.

- Thick curtains reduce heat loss in the winter and can be drawn on extremely hot summer days to prevent overheating.

- Shutters fitted outside provide extra heat control.

- A high-performance combustion stove warms the room in winter and makes it cosy and comfortable. Conducted heat vents have a greater heat output than conventional open fires, while complete combustion and filters minimize the emission of pollutants. The chimney is checked for cracks and swept every year to keep it working efficiently and safely.

- The television and sound system are switched off to conserve energy when they are not in use.

Floors

Consider all the options when choosing the best type of floor for your living area. Floors need to be tough and easy to clean, but the ideal choice depends on your circumstances. A single person may find that

WIPE YOUR FEET
When you come indoors, it takes a minimum of eight steps to remove dirt from the soles of your shoes.

taking out the vacuum cleaner once a week is enough to keep a carpet clean and looking good, while a mother of three young children may curse a carpet and find a timber floor, which can be wiped or swept clean so quickly, a blessing. The question of comfort is also subjective, depending on climate and personal preference.

Tips for keeping your floor clean

Whichever material you choose for your floor, it will last longer if you clean it regularly and give vulnerable spots some protection. Consider these measures:

- Place door mats at all entrances, inside and out.
- Position rugs where spills are likely, such as by the sink or fridge.
- Place other protectors such as glides and covers under furniture.
- Avoid walking on the floors with high heels.
- Lift rather than slide furniture across floors.

Cleaning timber floors

Sweep timber floors regularly, mop spills with a dry cloth or paper towel, and remove sticky patches with a damp cloth. The basic rule of thumb is sweep first, mop second. Water alone will remove light soiling and is fine for frequent cleaning.

For a tougher clean, you will need to consider the type of finish or sealer on your timber floor, as each benefits from slightly different treatments.

Oil-finished timber Sweep, then clean an oil-finished timber floor with a damp mop. Wash with 1 part methylated spirits (denatured alcohol) to 10 parts hot water. Mop spills with a dry, clean cloth and remove sticky foods with a warm damp cloth. To remove sticky food from an oil-finished timber floor, sprinkle an absorbent powder (talcum powder or flour) over it, then wipe with a warm, damp cloth.

If you wish to polish an oil-finished floor, use a liquid acrylic and spirit-based wax polish rather than an oil-impregnated mop.

Polyurethane finish Mop sparingly with hot water alone or a mild soap or detergent solution. Avoid letting the wood become too wet. About once a month, mop with a mixture of 1 part methylated spirits (denatured alcohol) to 10 parts water. Rinse with a clean, damp mop. Buff with a dry cloth tied to the end of a broom. A timber floor finished with polyurethane needs sanding and resurfacing every few years.

Wax polish finish Brush off dust and debris regularly and wipe over with a damp mop or cloth to remove sticky and oily stains. Polish and clean with liquid acrylic and spirit-based wax polish. To avoid a build-up of polish (which will eventually have to be removed), apply the polish sparingly only where it is needed, such as heavy traffic areas, and don't apply too much.

Removing stains and scratches from timber floors

When it comes to removing stains from timber floors, they fall into two main categories: floors with hard finishes and those without. In the group with hard finishes are polyurethane and other varnishes; in the second group are natural finish, wax finish and penetrating stains. If you're not sure which finish you're dealing with, take a closer look at the stain you are trying to remove. If it appears to be in the finish, the wood probably does have a hard finish. If it's in the wood, it very likely does not have a hard finish.

Alternatively, drop a little water on the flooring. If it makes a white mark, it is without a hard finish. The mark will disappear when the water dries.

HIGH HEEL DAMAGE ON FLOORS
The Hoover Book of Home Management, 1963, has the following advice about minimizing damage wrought by the then fashionable stiletto-heeled shoe: 'A tactful way with visitors is to have a supply of tiny plastic heel guards at the ready for those sharp high heels...'. Consider this: a 57 kg (125 lb) woman in high heels exerts 900 kg per 6.5 cm^2 (2000 lb per 1 inch^2) at each step.

Restoring timber floors

DAMAGE	WITHOUT HARD FINISH	WITH HARD FINISH
Scratch	Wax	Touch up kit (available from a flooring retailer)
Food	Clean up with a damp cloth, rub dry, then wax	Use a specialized cleaner
Chewing gum, crayon, candle wax	Apply ice, or iron over an ink blotter. Use a solvent-based wax to loosen	Ice or specialized cleaner
Oil and greasy stains	Rub with kitchen soap, or saturate cotton with hydrogen peroxide and cover stain with cotton, then saturate second piece of cotton with ammonia and place over the first. Repeat. Dry and buff	Specialized cleaner
Cigarette burn	Shallow burn: rub with fine sandpaper or steel wool moistened with wax. Deep burn: remove charred parts, rub with fine sandpaper, stain, wax and buff	Shallow burn: touch up kit comprising stain and refinish. Deep burn: replace individual planks
Water mark (and white spots)	Fine steel wool and wax, then fine sandpaper. Clean with fine wool and mineral spirits. Dry, stain, wax and buff	Not usually a problem
Water mark (dark spots)	Try above. Household bleach or vinegar. Soak for 1 hour. Rinse with damp cloth, dry. Fine sandpaper, stain, wax and buff	Specialized cleaner with scrub pad
Mould on timber	Wood cleaner	Specialized cleaner and a scrub pad if stubborn
Heel marks	Rub wax in with fine steel wool and hand buff to return shine	Rub wax in with fine steel wool and hand buff to return shine

Fixing a bouncing floorboard

The brick piers holding up the bearers and joists under the floor were probably originally laid on a lime mortar bed. Over time the mortar has worn slightly or the piers have sunk, creating a gap between the bearer and the pier. This causes the bounce, and it needs to be packed. You will need to go under the house to do this job.

1 You can buy load-bearing plastic wedges that will fill the gap between the pier and the bearer. Don't overpack the bearer or you'll end up with a high spot in the lounge.

2 Also, it's possible your bearers or joists around the perimeter of the room will slot into a cut-out in the brick wall. There is usually a gap underneath the bearer or joist in that slot that needs packing. If you pack the piers and not the perimeter you'll still have the bounce.

3 Get someone in the room to bounce up and down to check the job.

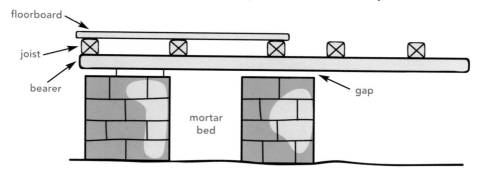

Fixing a creaking floorboard

You must understand the cause first. When two boards are tight together and have lifted slightly off the joist, you stand on one, and the board rubs on the other board as it goes down under your weight and creaks. So therefore there's movement, and you have to secure that board and stop it from moving.

CARPET OVER FLOORBOARDS

1 If you have no plans for polishing the floorboards and there's carpet, carefully lift the carpet.

2 Using a countersunk screw head, screw the boards down where it creaks.

POLISHED FLOORBOARDS

1 For a creaking polished board you will need to gain access under the floor.

2 Find the creak under the floor. There should be a tiny gap between the underside of the floorboard and the top of the joist.

Have some small wooden wedges ready. Squirt wood glue all over each wedge and in the gap, and tap them in. Don't overtap the wedges as they will cause the board to lift.

Fixing a squeaking stair tread

If your stairs are squeaking it means there is movement in one of your treads. You will need to get under your stairs — most sets have access.

1 Underneath you will see your two stringers, which are the long timbers running down either side of the stairs.

2 You'll also see housed-out sections in the shape of stairs on each stringer. The risers and treads sit in these house-outs, with timber wedges keeping them in place.

3 Squirt some woodwork glue around the loose wedge and tap it in until it's tight. This will tighten up the tread and get rid of the squeak.

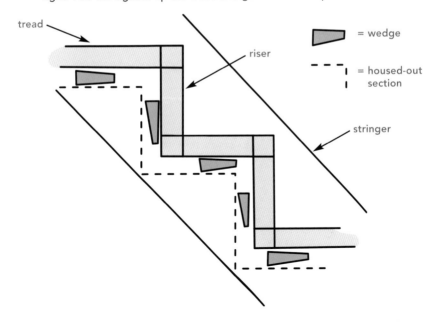

tread

riser

= wedge

= housed-out section

stringer

Removing stains from lino and vinyl floors

Quick action is always best: wipe, mop and scoop spills as soon as possible. Avoid using undiluted bleach (it may cause yellowing) and abrasive cleaners (they can scratch or dull the surface). If you are left with stains, try the following.

- Wipe the stain with an all-purpose cleaner.

- Try a pencil eraser.

- Use lemon and salt for rust stains — cut a lemon in half, sprinkle with plenty of salt and rub in the stain. Using a rag or sponge, rinse with water.

- For thick grease or tar, try mineral spirits, but use it with caution, testing on a tiny portion first as mineral spirits can take the shine off. Another way to remove tar is to cool it with an ice cube and pry it off with a spatula when it is brittle.

- A bleach solution made of 2 cups water and ¼ cup chlorine bleach will remove many stains including beer, wine and other alcoholic drinks, coffee, tomato sauce and mustard. Organic stains such as blood, grass stains and pet accidents can be treated with this solution or lemon juice, or lemon and salt.

How to clean your carpet

To protect your carpets, use doormats, preferably one inside and one outside each entrance point. This removes a great deal of dirt that would otherwise get walked onto the carpet. Always wipe your feet and train others to do so too. Some families habitually remove their shoes on

THREE GOLDEN RULES OF CARPET CARE
Manufacturers recommend regular care to keep your carpet looking its best:
1 Vacuum at least once a week, more often in heavy traffic areas.
2 Get working on spills and stains immediately.
3 Wet clean every 1 to 2 years or as needed.

BUBBLE AID
Liquid spills can be treated by sparingly pouring on soda water or mineral water. The bubbles cause the spillage to rise to the surface where it can be quickly blotted.

entering the home and this keeps floors cleaner as well as looking good for longer. Place castors and protectors under furniture legs to help prevent the pile from being crushed.

In a dirty carpet, the soil embedded at the base of the tufts grinds away at the fibre, gradually wearing it down. So vacuuming regularly is not just about keeping up with the Jones's clean appearance. Keeping the carpet clean also prolongs its life. Carpet sweepers remove crumbs and other surface dirt, while vacuum cleaners pull out the dirt from deeper down. When tougher action is called for, there are several options to choose from: spot treatments, carpet shampoos and cleaners, and carpet-cleaning machines.

Caring for valuable or delicate rugs and carpets

Delicate rugs and carpets, such as antique ones, need special treatment.

- Vacuum delicate rugs with reduced suction, using the gentlest power on your cleaner.
- If you don't have a vacuum cleaner with adjustable power, adjust it yourself by placing a screen of plastic on the nozzle or even on the carpet itself.
- Vacuum slowly in the direction of the pile.
- Avoid wet cleaning.

THROW SALT OVER YOUR SHOULDER BUT NOT ON RED WINE
It is said that salt heaped liberally over a spill of red wine will soak it up and save the stain. But professional carpet cleaners do not recommend it on carpets. Instead they suggest a combination of white wine and methylated spirits (denatured alcohol).

On the spot: A to Z of carpet stains

Most stains can be treated in one of three ways, or a combination. Familiarize yourself with each of the three methods, then use the list below to find and treat your particular problem.

■ **Treatment A** Mild detergent (1 teaspoon neutral detergent — that is, no alkalis or bleaches — in 1 cup lukewarm water).

■ **Treatment B** Vinegar solution ($\frac{1}{3}$ cup white vinegar in $\frac{2}{3}$ cup water).

■ **Treatment C** Ammonia solution (1 tablespoon household ammonia in $\frac{1}{2}$ cup water).

Stain removal

STAIN	REMOVAL METHOD
Ballpoint pen	Sponge with a dry cloth and methylated spirits (denatured alcohol), or a small amount of dry-cleaning solvent, before sponging with Treatment A. Finally sponge with clean water
Beer	Sponge with Treatment A, followed by Treatment B, before sponging with clean water
Blood	Blot with cloth or paper towel. Use cold water, working it into the pile. Blot again and repeat as necessary. Small amounts of blood should come out fairly easily. If this does not work, try the following steps: sponge with Treatment A, then Treatment C, then sponge rinse with cold water
Butter	Sponge with a small amount of dry-cleaning solvent, then sponge with Treatment A
Chewing gum	As for butter
Chocolate	Sponge with Treatment A, followed by Treatment C. Repeat with Treatment A before sponging with clean water
Coffee	As for beer
Cola drinks	As for beer
Crayons	Sponge sparingly with dry-cleaning solvent, followed by Treatment A. Finally, sponge with clean water
Dirt	As for chocolate
Egg (raw)	As for beer

STAIN	REMOVAL METHOD
Food	Remove excess then wipe with cloth wrung out with Treatment A
Food colouring	Professional carpet cleaner
Fruit juice and fruit	As for beer
Furniture polish	As for crayons
Glue (white craft)	Sponge with Treatment A, followed by Treatment B, then Treatment A again. Finally, sponge with clean water
Gravy	As for crayons
Ice cream	As for chocolate
Ink	Blot excess. Natural inks such as Indian ink are very difficult to remove
Iodine	Sponge with Treatment A, followed by Treatment C, then Treatment B and finally Treatment A again. Finish with clean water
Lily pollen	If dry, vacuum excess. If wet, soak up with dry cloths
Milk	As for chocolate
Mud	Let it dry completely first, then brush with a stiff brush to break it up. Finally, vacuum
Nail polish	Use non-oily polish remover on a cloth for small stains, then sponge with Treatment A. Finally, sponge with clean water
Paint	While still wet, emulsion can be rinsed off with water. If dry, break up the paint with the edge of a blunt knife and then vacuum. To remove gloss, use sparing amounts of mineral spirits but be warned, it can remove colour from carpet. When dry, for a superficial stain, try shaving off the paint with a sharp knife — only try it if you are confident of a steady hand, otherwise you may risk holes
Pen (marker)	As for crayons
Red wine	Blot with paper towel or a dry cloth. Sprinkle with white wine, which is acidic, to neutralize the stain, or water, and blot again. Remove the remaining stain with a clean cloth and methylated spirits (denatured alcohol)

Stain removal

STAIN	REMOVAL METHOD
Rust	Put lemon juice on the mark, leave for 1 minute and rinse with water. Repeat if necessary
Shoe polish	As for crayons
Soft drinks	As for glue (white craft)
Soot	As soot is oily, do not attempt to remove it with water and detergents. Vacuum as much away as possible and tackle small stains with a solvent cleaner
Soy sauce	Sponge with Treatment A, followed by Treatment C, before sponging with clean water
Tar or oil	Remove with a spirit-based cleaner
Tea	Using a paper towel or dry absorbent cloth, blot as much as possible. Add a little water and soak up again until the colour is gone. You can also safely try Treatment A or methylated spirits (denatured alcohol) dabbed on the residue. Alternatively, try sponging with Treatment A, followed by Treatment B, before sponging with clean water
Urine (dried stain)	Sponge with Treatment A, followed by Treatment B, then Treatment C, then Treatment A again. To finish, sponge with clean water
Urine (wet stain)	Blot, then sponge with clean water. Sponge with Treatment C, followed by Treatment A. Finally sponge with clean water
Vomit	Scoop and blot as much as possible
Water stains	Professional help only
Wax	As for crayons
White wine	As for glue (white craft)

- Do not use valuable carpets in areas of high traffic or in doorways where they are likely to receive harsher, dirtier treatment.

- For serious spillages, blot and gently scrape as much as you can, then wrap the carpet tightly in plastic to avoid drying the stain. This helps prevent it setting. Whisk it off to a professional cleaner.

- When storing valuable carpets and rugs, you should roll rather than fold, and roll pile-side out to prevent wearing.

- If storing delicate or antique rugs, line them with acid-free paper before rolling and place in acid-free boxes.

Doors

There are a few common door problems that can usually be easily fixed by the home handyperson.

Fixing a sliding door

If the sliding door is fairly old, it's probably the case that the nylon wheel of the roller has worn out and needs to be replaced. Sliding doors have two rollers on the underside of the door. These can be adjusted to either raise or lower the door. At each edge down the bottom of an aluminium sliding door there's a hole with an adjustment screw. This will raise or lower the roller and do the same to the door. You can line up your lock doing this or simply square up the door.

1 Remove the door by lifting it up and pulling it out at the bottom. The door will come out at the bottom track and then drop down out of the top track.

2 The rollers are in a channel at the bottom of the door and can usually just be levered out with a screw-driver. There are many types of rollers, so take them with you to the hardware store so you can buy the right replacement rollers.

3 Put the new ones in, then replace the door. Put the top into the top track first, then do the bottom.

4 Adjust to suit your lock.

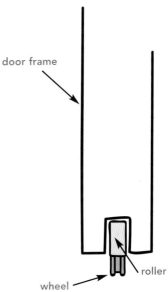

door frame

roller

wheel

Fixing a door that doesn't close properly

There are a few causes. Poorly fitted, loose hinges, swelling, and continuous painting over the years of the door and jamb can cause the door to catch.

Loose hinges

Hopefully, it's the hinges. This is the easiest to fix. Usually the top hinge has loosened on the door or the jamb under the weight and movement. Try tightening the screws.

1 You'll probably find the holes have been stripped, so take out one screw at a time and slot in one or two regular matches (depending on the size of the hole).

2 Snap off the excess and replace the screw. This will tighten the hinges, pull the door back up and create the gap required for the door to close smoothly.

Swollen or overpainted door

If the door is swollen or overpainted, then you'll have to plane the door off.

1 Before you remove the door, use a pencil to mark out the area and depth of the sections to be planed.

2 Remove the door and stand it up on the ground in a door clamp (just a piece of 100- x 50-mm/4- x 2-inch timber with a cut-out slot that's a bit bigger than the width of the door). Slot a wedge in with the door to keep it stable. The wedge can be wood, or even a chisel.

3 Remove the latch so that the plane doesn't get damaged, and plane the door down carefully so it will fit into the door frame.

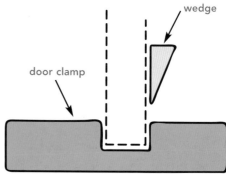

wedge

door clamp

Fixing a door sticking at the bottom

A door sticking at the bottom is normally caused by hinges dropping or, on external doors, damp penetration at the base could cause the wood to swell and expand. The door will need to be removed and re-hung or excess planed from the bottom. Alternatively, an uneven floor surface may cause this problem, and changing normal butt hinges to rising butts should clear it up.

When a door is sticking at the bottom it is best to use a scribing technique to measure how much wood needs to be removed in order to ease movement:

1   Put the door in a closed position. Cut a block of wood with a height representing the required clearance between the bottom of the door and the floor.

2   Hold a pencil tight on top of the block, with its point resting on the block edge. Draw the block and pencil across the floor surface at the base of the door, leaving a pencil guideline along the bottom of the door.

3   The door may now be removed from its hinges and trimmed to this guideline. For small cuts a wood plane may be used. For larger sections, a jigsaw is the ideal tool.

4   Re-hang the door once the wood has been removed.

Fixing a door sticking at the sides

A door sticking at the sides is more often than not caused by paint build-up over the years. Planing is therefore all that is required. Alternatively, it may be down to hinge movement and the door may need to be re-hung.

Fixing a rattling door

A rattling door may be a perfect fit in terms of its position in the jamb, with the actual problem relating to the position of the doorstop. In other words, the doorstop has been positioned too far from the latch, so that even small gusts of wind or draughts cause the door latch to rattle rather than being held firmly in place by the latch position and doorstop combined. Conversely, the door may not close properly, because the doorstop is positioned too far forward or too close to the catch plate, and therefore the door cannot physically be shut in place. Draught exclusion stripping can be added to rebated jambs to alleviate much of the rattling, whereas plant-on doorstops can be repositioned easily.

1 Remove the doorstop by carefully levering it out of position using an old chisel to assist you.

2 Close the door and mark a line on the door lining to show where the ideal position for the edge of the doorstop will be, to allow the door to close tightly but still easily.

3 Simply reopen the door and nail the doorstop back in place according to the new guidelines. It may also be necessary to move the doorstop on the head and hinged side of the frame, so check for this once the first piece of doorstop has been repositioned.

Fixing a stiff lock or keyhole

The first thing everyone thinks of for a stiff lock or key hole is WD 40, sewing machine oil or grease. These may work for a short time but not for long. They attract dust and dirt, and will clog up the mechanism and make it stiff again.

What you need is some graphite. You can buy it in a fine powder form. It comes in a plastic container with a pointed nozzle.

1 Squirt the graphite on the key as well as into the key hole.

2 For a deadlock or door handle you may have to pull the lock or handle off and squirt the graphite into the lock.

3 The latch on the edge of the door is a separate unit to the handle. Squirt it with graphite as well so the whole action can move smoothly.

Caring for painted walls and ceilings

- Dust occasionally with either a soft attachment on the vacuum cleaner, a broom with a soft cloth tied onto the brush or a dry cloth. Start at the ceiling and work down.

- Spot-clean regularly to keep walls looking good. Scuffs at door entrances, finger marks near light fittings and door handles, and sticky finger marks at child height on the wall are the hot spots. A railing on both sides of the stairs is one way to prevent finger marks appearing by the walls up stairwells. To spot clean, try (in order of most gentle method first) a damp, clean, colourfast cloth; a clean cloth dipped in a mild dishwashing detergent solution or a cream cleanser.

- Regularly remove cobwebs from the ceiling and give corners a brush with a long-handled broom covered in a soft cloth, or a long-handled duster. Washing the ceiling is a messy job, involving drips and buckets of water. It may be something you feel you only really need to do before painting but, on the other hand, a good clean can be almost as revitalizing as painting, especially if the ceiling has been discoloured by mould.

Filling small holes or cracks in plaster walls

1 Remove any loose debris and dust from the hole or crack in your wall with a scraper and cut it back to form a V-shaped groove, which will give the filler a stronger surface to adhere to.

2 Apply multipurpose or masonry filler with a filling knife so that it sits proud of the hole in the wall. It is important to do this because it will eventually shrink back slightly as it begins to dry.

3 Once the filler has dried (after about 20 minutes) completely sand the surface smooth by using medium-grade abrasive paper wrapped around a sanding block.

4 Deep holes, such as those that will be left when wall plugs are removed, can be plugged using scrunched-up newspaper before filling.

Filling small holes in plasterboard

1 Begin by using a knife to cut away any loose areas of plaster that are crumbling away.

2 Use scissors to cut some fibreglass plaster repair tape into a number of small pieces. Then apply the repair tape in overlapping layers so that they completely cover the hole.

3 Apply filler over the repair tape. Allow to dry, then sand smooth.

Filling a crack in the ceiling

Cracks in plasterboard ceilings generally follow the edges of the plasterboard sheets, and are caused by movement in the ceiling structure as temperature and humidity changes. In lath-and-plaster ceilings, the cracks may be irregular or run parallel to the laths to which the plaster is bonded.

HPL

1 Draw the blade of a trimming knife along the crack, undercutting each edge slightly so that the filler will be locked in place when it sets. Then use an old paintbrush to brush any dust from the crack. On lath-and-plaster ceilings, brush some water along the crack to stop the dry plaster from sucking moisture out of the filler and making it crack as it sets.

2 Load up a filling knife with filler and press it well into the crack, drawing the blade across it as you work. After filling a short section of crack in this way, draw the knife blade along the crack to smooth the filler level with the surrounding surface. Carry on in this way until you have filled the whole crack. Allow the filler to set hard, then sand the repair smooth and redecorate to conceal it.

Painting tips

Painting your home's interior, though very exciting, can be a daunting task. With a little know-how, however, and some handy tips, you'll be amazed at the professional finish you will achieve, with the least amount of disruption.

- When selecting a paintbrush, do not compromise on quality. A good-quality brush should have a strong hardwood handle, a copper or nickel-plated steel ferrule, and pure or synthetic tapered bristles with fledged ends (like the split ends of hair).

- Before painting, apply a barrier cream to your hands. This will keep the skin moist and make it easier to remove the paint. When you have finished painting, always clean your hands (especially before eating), but try to avoid using solvents to do this as they will dry out the skin.

- To avoid being overcome with the strong fumes of paint or solvents, provide plenty of ventilation to the room you are going to work in. Keep doors and windows open or, if this is not possible because of wind or rain, use electric fans.

- Avoid smoking while working with solvents or amid strong vapours because the heat from the cigarette is enough to increase the toxicity in the chemical breakdown, making these vapours even more dangerous.

HOW MUCH PAINT TO BUY

To work out how much paint you should buy, calculate the total surface area to be painted. The surface area of a wall is obtained when you multiply its length by its height. For example, a 4- x 5-m (13- x 16½-foot) wall has a surface area of 20 sq m (215 square feet). Before buying your paint, check on the can to see how much coverage it will give. Keep in mind, however, that this is only a rough indication, as the application method and the type of surface being painted are more likely to dictate the amount of paint you will use.

- When painting either large or small surfaces, always paint the edges first.

- On narrow vertical areas, such as doors, start at the top and work your way down.

- On horizontal surfaces, start at the point furthest away from you, and work your way across. Do not start in the middle.

- For best results and a more even coverage, apply the paint in a criss-cross fashion, using the flat of the brush. This technique is called 'crows nesting'.

- Try to refrain from brushing over too large an area each time you fill your brush. You will only end up with an uneven finish and be disappointed with the result.

- To load a brush with paint, dip the brush into the paint can no more than one-third the length of the bristles. Lift the bristles out of the paint and gently tap the inside of the can three or four times with the tip of both sides of the brush to remove the excess paint.

- To load a roller with paint, place the roller in the paint and roll it firmly back and forth along the tray. Make every effort to load paint evenly onto the roller as this will prevent paint dripping when the roller is lifted from the tray to the surface. If too much paint is left on the sleeve, it will drip and tend to skid over the surface.

Painting walls

Walls should be carefully prepared before repainting. Flaws and imperfections should be filled and sanded, and ideally bare plaster should be sized and papered. If you prefer to paint directly onto new plaster, then seal it first with a multi-surface primer to prevent it from absorbing excess paint. Previously painted surfaces should be wiped down with sugar soap solution to remove dirt and grease, and any rough patches or holes should be filled and sanded. Strong, dark paint colours and highly patterned wallpapers are particularly difficult to cover with lighter paint colours. It is advisable to paint a coat of white multipurpose primer before applying the new colour in such cases. Painting rooms in different colour combinations is a very popular look. Many people like picking out 'feature walls' in different colours. Internal corners where two colours meet can be difficult to paint neatly, particularly if the walls are not completely perpendicular. It is best to wait for one colour to dry, then mask it off with low-tack masking tape, and paint the second colour.

1   Prepare previously painted walls by washing them down with sugar soap.

2   Load a small paintbrush (for example, 5 cm/2 inches) by dipping the bristles about halfway into the paint then wipe off excess on the edge of the tin or paint kettle. 'Cut in' around the edges of the room. Treat each wall as a panel, working the colour into the corners. Mask off the top of the skirting boards if you do not feel confident about painting freehand up to the edge. Use masking tape around obstacles such as light switches to protect them.

3   Use a roller or large brush to fill in, painting one wall at a time. You may find it easiest if you work from the top to the bottom and to start in the top right-hand corner, which will prevent you brushing against areas that you have just painted (reverse this if you are left-handed). This is not a hard and fast rule, however. Allow the paint to dry and then apply a second coat using the same method.

Painting a ceiling

If painting a previously painted ceiling wipe it down first with a solution of sugar soap using a sponge or long-handled mop. Seal stubborn stains with primer.

1   If possible, clear the room of all its furniture and protect the floor with a fabric or plastic dustsheet. If necessary tape this to the skirting board with

masking tape to prevent it from moving. Begin by 'cutting in' with a small paintbrush. If you have coving do not worry if you overpaint the edges slightly because coving is usually finished in satinwood or gloss paint so this will be painted over later anyway. If you have an unpainted plaster cornice, you can protect it with masking tape.

2 Mask off pendant light fittings and paint around them. If you are having difficulties painting close up to the ceiling rose, switch the electricity supply off at the fuse box and then remove the plastic rose with a small screwdriver, which will expose the backplate and the wiring.

3 When cutting in is complete fill in the remaining ceiling area with a roller or a large brush. Fix an extension pole onto a standard roller cage, in order to reach high ceilings, or use a step ladder. Allow the first coat to dry before applying a second coat.

Painting skirting boards (and woodwork)

1 Prepare previously painted skirting boards by rubbing them down with a flexible sanding pad — this will key the surface, giving the new paint something to adhere to. Use a damp cloth to wipe away dust before applying new paint.

2 Protect the floor with a plastic sheet taped to the floor just below the skirting (if the room is carpeted, slip a piece of stiff card between the carpet and skirting). Use a piece of card held against the wall while you paint the skirting board using a small paintbrush.

Wallpaper

Washable wallpapers are coated with a thin, transparent vinyl layer, which makes them easier to clean and more difficult to stain. Dust them regularly with a soft brush and wipe over with a damp cloth dipped in mild detergent and warm water. Rinse with a damp cloth and a bucket of clean warm water.

Non-washable wallpaper requires gentler treatment. Dust regularly with a soft brush or cloth. Spot-clean by dabbing with powdered borax and brushing out. Another homemade remedy is to rub gently with a piece of bread rolled into a ball, or a soft rubber eraser.

Stripping old wallpaper

1 Use a scraping knife or wire brush to make slits all over the surface of the existing wallpaper.

2 Fill an electric steam stripper with water to the level that is indicated on it and then switch the power on.

3 Then hold the plate of the wallpaper stripper carefully over one section of the papered surface until you can see that it is beginning to blister and bubble.

4 Slide the scraping knife underneath the bubbling paper. Then carefully remove the paper in strips — it should come away easily by this stage.

5 Finish by removing any residue that is left on the wall by soaking a sponge in warm water and wiping the surface down.

How to hang wallpaper

1 Measure the drop from the ceiling to the skirting and add a couple of centimetres (about an inch) top and bottom to provide an overlap. If you are working with patterned wallpaper, take the repeat into account. Cut the first few lengths and lay them on the pasting table. Paste carefully, from the centre of the paper outwards, with the edge overlapping the table slightly to avoid getting paste on the face of the paper.

2 Making sure that the first drop of wallpaper is hung straight is vital and, as most walls are not completely square, you will need a plumb line. Choose a point in the room that is close to the darkest corner and measure just under a width of the wallpaper away from the corner. Hold the string at the top of the wall, let the plumb fall to the skirting and wait until it has completely stopped moving. Then mark with a pencil at intervals along the string. Join up the line with a metal straightedge.

3 Starting at the top, smooth the paper onto the wall, allowing an overlap of a couple of centimetres (about an inch). Work down the length using a decorator's brush to smooth the paper from the centre outwards, squeezing out any air bubbles. The paper should be worked well into the corner and overlap the adjacent wall by about 1 cm ($\frac{1}{2}$ inch).

4 Use the rounded tip of a pair of decorator's scissors in order to crease the paper carefully at the point where it meets the ceiling. Slowly pull the wallpaper away from the wall at the top and use the scissors to trim away the excess. Then carefully smooth the paper back down the wall using a decorator's brush. Repeat the process at the point where the wall meets the skirting board.

5 Hang the second drop of paper by carefully aligning it with the edge of the first drop and sliding it up against it to achieve a 'butt' joint (the two edges should meet without any trace of a gap at all). If you are using a patterned wallpaper, then you will need to slide the paper along the wall until the two halves of the pattern meet up at the correct position.

REMOVING CHILDREN'S MARKS FROM WALLS

Wax crayon

■ For hard, non-porous surfaces such as glass, use mineral spirits or powder detergent on a soft cloth and rub gently using small, circular strokes.

■ For wooden furniture, use a strong all-purpose cleaner and soft cloth.

■ For varnished and painted woodwork, brick and stone, brush with a nail brush dipped in dry-cleaning solution. Then mix dry-cleaning solution with powder detergent and rub again. Rinse with clean water and dry.

■ For carpet and soft furnishings, rub or press the mark with dry-cleaning solution, probably a few times, using a clean cloth or paper towel. If any colour remains, try a very mild bleach solution, but test a small area first.

■ For wallpaper, use a pencil eraser then an all-purpose liquid cleaner.

Liquid paint

For varnished and painted woodwork and painted walls, try dabbing with a damp cloth. If this fails, try powder detergent and a damp cloth, but be careful of glossy surfaces as they may become scratched or dull. Finally, try nail polish remover.

Chalk

■ On wallpaper, use a damp cloth and a liquid cleaning solution or household soap. If that doesn't work, try rubbing with an eraser.

■ On brick or stone, brush with a stiff-bristled brush then scrub with a paste cleaner or powdered detergent and water.

■ On vinyl flooring or desk surfaces, use a liquid cleaner.

6 Trim the top and bottom of the paper as shown in step 4. Repeat the process around the whole room. Make sure that the last drop of paper overlaps the corner by approximately 1 cm (1/2 inch) and is pushed well into the corner using the decorator's brush. Finally, finish off by wiping away any wallpaper paste that may have been left on the ceiling or cornice and skirting board using a clean, damp sponge.

Furniture

Your living room furniture is an investment that needs to be treated with care and respect to ensure it remains in optimum condition for as long as possible.

Cleaning and caring for wooden furniture

- Lacquered furniture can also be wiped with a damp duster using a fine water mist spray on the duster to avoid getting the wood too wet. Dry with a second cloth and buff with a soft cloth. While it is not necessary to polish lacquered furniture, an occasional application brings a shine to a dull surface.

- Regular waxing of waxed furniture helps protect it from heat and moisture. Once or twice a year should be sufficient. Solid wax produces better results even though it's harder to apply.

- Be sure to protect tabletops and other wooden surfaces by sticking felt underneath ornaments and using coasters or mats to protect surfaces from the heat of cups or liquid from vases.

Removing stains and marks from wooden furniture

Inevitably, wooden furniture will suffer the occasional mishap. When attempting to remedy marks and stains, proceed with caution, starting with the mildest methods first. Try repeated gentle methods rather than one harsh treatment. While there are many commercial products available, it is worth trying home remedies first, but make sure you work in a well-ventilated place.

- **Greasy finger marks** Wipe with a just-damp cloth that has been wrung in a mild solution of soap flakes. Dry thoroughly.

- **Heat marks** White marks may indicate that the finish has been damaged. Try burnishing out the mark with a cream metal polish, rubbing it briskly in the same direction as the grain. Follow with a polish of wax. Do small sections at a time, wiping the polish away as you go.

- **Rough patch** Smooth with very fine steel wool dipped in liquid wax polish. Proceed with great caution on veneered surfaces.

- **Water marks** Try removing marks left by wet glasses as you would heat marks (see above).

- **Scratches** Mask light scratches with a similar coloured wax crayon or shoe polish. Leave it to absorb before buffing briskly.

- **Alcohol spots** Burnish with a cream metal finish, rubbing briskly in the direction of the grain. Follow with a light wax polish.

Cleaning and caring for fabric upholstery

All upholstery benefits from a regular vacuum to remove dust and other debris that finds its way into crevices. Preventative measures, some more fashionable than others, include the following:

- Soil repellents and stain repellents work by making spills bead up rather than soak into the fabric.

- Antimacassars are coverings thrown over the back of sofas and chairs to protect them from grease in the hair. Typically, these take the form of small lacy circles or rectangles.

- Throws are particularly handy for protecting upholstery from the rigours of pets and young children.

- Loose covers may be laundered.

- Arm guards and back guards protect the most vulnerable spots on chairs and sofas.

Cleaning and caring for leather upholstery

To spot-clean minor stains, wipe leather upholstery with a little water, taking care not to get the leather too damp. To more thoroughly clean leather upholstery, dust, then use saddle soap or a similar product. Let it

SHAMPOOING FABRIC UPHOLSTERY

Like carpet fibres, upholstery fabric is generally worn away by dirt. Regular shampooing — perhaps once a year or even once every 2 years — helps to keep sofas and similar items of furniture clean.

Loose covers are usually designed to be washed, but check the care labels. If in doubt about shrinkage, wash the covers in cold water and replace them on the furniture when they are still slightly damp.

Hand-shampooing is good for delicate, dirty upholstery. You should follow the manufacturer's instructions on a commercial shampoo. In general, it's best to use a soft brush dipped in the foam made by a shampoo. Rinse by wiping the foam off with a well-wrung cloth dipped in clean water. Dry thoroughly, then vacuum.

For furniture with fixed upholstery, you might consider a home steam-extraction machine which pumps liquid into the fabric and sucks it out again, eliminating the problem of wet seats, arms and cushions, which take forever to dry. Even so, good ventilation helps speed up the drying time.

dry thoroughly before using the furniture again. If the leather is beginning to crack or seems dry, use a leather conditioner but test in an inconspicuous spot for its effect on colour.

Windows

Most old houses have problems with windows that won't open. Usually you'll find that they are either painted shut, swollen or nailed shut.

Painted shut

1 If the window is painted shut, get yourself a Stanley knife and carefully cut the paint in the corner of the stop bead (the small beading that holds the window in) and sash.

2 Using a block of timber and a hammer, place the timber on the window frame and very gently go around and tap the frame of the window. Then jemmy the window up.

Swollen shut

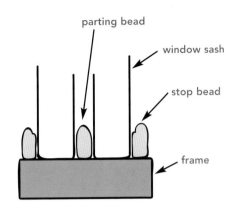

1 If the window is swollen, it needs to come out. Remove the stop beads. You'll be able to remove the window with the sash cords still attached. If you break a stop bead, just buy some more.

2 Run a plane and a bit of sandpaper up the sides of the window and clean up the offending edges.

3 Replace the window and make sure it goes up and down smoothly.

4 Replace the stop beads.

Nailed shut

1 If the window is nailed shut, find the nails and dig out a bit of the timber around the heads to expose them.

2 Pull out the nails with pliers or pinchers.

3 Putty up the holes, then paint.

Fixing a flyscreen

1 Remove the flyscreen and lay it on a table. On the inside of the frame is a little rebate. The screen is held in there with a small rubber hose. Find the join in the hose and prise one end out with a screwdriver. Get hold of the end and pull everything out.

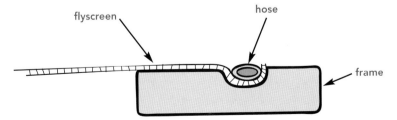

2 Lay the new screen over the frame, allowing about 5 cm (2 inches) extra all the way around. Start with one side and poke the hose into the rebate. This will lock the screen into the rebate. To make life easy you can buy a special wheel to do this. Don't tension your screen too much as it'll bow in your frame. If you're left with a crease, just pull it out and start again.

3 Now trim off the excess with a Stanley knife.

Window treatments

Curtains, blinds and shutters not only enhance the decorative effect of your living area, they also make it more energy efficient, keeping excess heat and harsh light out during summer and helping to prevent heat loss during winter.

Cleaning blinds

- Dust blinds regularly.

- To refresh the colour, wipe linen blinds with a cloth wrung out in methylated spirits (denatured alcohol) and vinegar, then wipe with a dry cloth.

- To remove stains, rub with a piece of bread.

- To wash a really dirty roller blind, take down the blind, keeping it rolled up but leaving the roller. Wet the blind and leave it for a few minutes. Give it a bath in warm water and detergent by gradually unrolling the blind and sponging it as you draw it into the bath. Keep going until you reach the end but do not dip the spring part. Rinse in the same gradual fashion. Let it drip on the clothesline for a few minutes then place on a towel on a table and dry from one end to the other with a second towel.

TO REVIVE VELVET CURTAINS

Dust makes velvet and plush curtains dull as well as enticing for dust mites. Go over with a brush of medium stiffness — against the pile for velvet and with the pile for plush — then hang in the bathroom over a hot bath to revive the pile.

Lighting

Choosing lighting is very much a personal decision, but do bear in mind that for a multifunction room, such as a living or family room, there will be lots of different lighting requirements that need to be addressed.

- Natural light is best, whether from windows, skylights and light tubes (small, highly efficient skylights). Keeping these clean allows more light to enter your home.

- Make the most of reflected light — pale-coloured ceilings, walls and furnishings bounce light around rooms, making the best use of daylight and artificial light. Use diffusers over lights, light-coloured shades, light tubes and skylights to spread light over large areas.

- Fluorescent lighting is the most efficient and is now available in a range of shapes and colours.

- A single, high-wattage bulb is much more efficient than a cluster of lower ones.

- Locate lights where you need them and use spot lights for reading, sewing and so on.

How to clean lampshades

Which cleaning method you use will depend on what material the lampshade is made of.

- **Fabric** Clean with a vacuum cleaner using the dusting brush attachment, adjusted to low power suction if possible. Attempt to clean spots with a mild detergent solution but be careful: you risk making water marks and/or dissolving the glue which holds the shade together.

- **Glass or plastic** Dust regularly. If necessary, wash with a clean cloth and detergent solution.

- **Paper and parchment** Brush often with a feather duster.

- **Raffia and straw** Vacuum with the brush attachment.

Replacing a fluorescent bulb

If your fluorescent light is completely dead, you'll need a new tube.

1 Before you start, go to your electrical box and turn the main switch OFF. Go inside, and check the other lights and any digital clocks to make sure you've hit the right switch.

2 Take the cover off the fluorescent light. Sometimes there are two screws at either end holding the caps on, which in turn hold the cover on. You should be able to take one off and pull the cover off to reveal the tube.

3 Grab the tube and rotate it slightly, pulling on it. The tube will pop out.

4 With the new tube, line up the lugs with the slot at each end. Slide the lugs in and rotate the tube. It is now locked off and ready to test.

5 The other thing that can go wrong with fluoros is the starter. These are small, white cylinders poking out from the light body. They look a bit like plastic film canisters, only smaller. If the new tube is in but the light is still flickering, you need to replace the starters.

6 Just push up slightly and turn the starter. It will pop out.

7 Replace it and see how you go. If you're still having problems, leave it at that and call an electrician.

THE IMPORTANCE OF SWEEPING CHIMNEYS

An annual clean sweep removes blockages, preventing poisonous gases from building up in the house. It also removes soot and creosote build-up, which if not cleared, can fuel serious fires.

Fireplaces

If you burn real coal and log fires, you should make sure that your chimneys are regularly swept by a professional who works to an authorized code of practice — otherwise soot will build up and may lead to a chimney fire. Smoky fires can be caused by the material you burn, such as damp logs, or perhaps through poor ventilation. Another reason can be the incorrect ratio of distances between the hearth, the chimney opening and the chimney top. This latter problem can only be remedied by a professional who may raise the hearth, add extra height to the chimney or put a baffle or shield on the front of the hearth.

To clean fireplace surrounds

1 Vacuum all loose soot and ash.

2 Rub off as much remaining soot as you can with a dry brush or cloth.

3 Wash the surround with a strong all-purpose cleaner recommended for the surface, whether it is brick, stone or marble. Alternatively, apply a weak solution of ammonia in water with a stiff brush.

4 Wash glass doors as you would any glass, unless the manufacturer's instructions advise otherwise.

Caring for home entertainment equipment

Remember to switch off and unplug all appliances before cleaning them.

- To remove greasy marks and other spots, use a cloth dampened with methylated spirits (denatured alcohol).

- To clean disc and tape compartments, wipe them out with a cloth. To reach the corners, use a cloth dampened with methylated spirits over a cotton bud.

- Clean the stylus of a record player by brushing dust off with a paint-brush. Dip the brush in methylated spirits (denatured alcohol) and brush gently again.

- To clean a TV screen, remove dust with a soft cloth, then wipe with a cloth dampened in either a glass-cleaning solution or warm water. Never spray directly onto the screen as this can cause damage.

- Clean VCR heads with a cleaning cassette (available from your local video hire store). A bad case may need professional cleaning. Regularly clean the VCR as dirty equipment damages tapes.

- Store your VCR in a cool, dry place, and avoid any sudden changes of temperature.

- Play and rewind VCR tapes at least once a year to redistribute tension evenly along the tape.

- Store CDs and DVDs in the cases provided, away from sunlight and direct heat.

- Hold each CD or DVD by the edge.

- Dust CDs and DVDs with a soft clean cloth, always wiping from the centre outwards. Do not wipe in a circular motion following the lines.

- To remove finger marks from CDs and DVDs, use a cloth dampened in mild detergent. If this does not restore the disc to full quality, try a little isopropyl alcohol (rubbing alcohol, available from chemists and some supermarkets).

Caring for your computer

- Place your computer where air can circulate around it.

- Do not expose it to long bursts of sunlight or direct heat.

- Do not store a computer in dusty or damp environments.

- Make sure the cables are not laid next to a heater, nor are likely to be tripped over.

THE HEALTHY HOME OFFICE

Whether it's a couple of pieces of furniture in the corner of the living room or a custom designed room, a home office has become a common feature of modern households. For a healthy home office, consider these factors.

- Make sure your desk chair is the correct height and gives adequate support to your lower back. Adjustable swivelling chairs with castors allow the most flexibility in movement and positioning.

- Ensure proper ventilation. A lot of office equipment emits gases such as ozone, which can worsen allergy symptoms.

- Turn off computers, photocopiers and printers when they are not in use as they produce ozone. If possible, put photocopiers in a separate room, as they are the worst ozone culprits.

- Ensure there is adequate lighting by placing the desk near a window, with the computer screen at right angles to the window. Set up a good desk lamp.

MAKE YOUR OWN ANTISTATIC CLOTH
Soak a lint-free cloth in fabric softener and water. Squeeze out the excess and dry the cloth before using it. You can use this cloth for cleaning.

- Do not move the computer when it is running as the hard disc is vulnerable to damage by jarring.
- Dust the screen and body of the computer with a damp, lint-free, soft cloth. Do not allow moisture to seep into any openings.
- Do not use alcohol or other solvents, abrasives or sprays of any kind when cleaning the computer.

To clean the keyboard

1 Turn the keyboard upside down to shift crumbs and dust. If you leave these particles to settle deeply, they may cause intermittent faults.

2 Turn the keyboard back the right way up and dust the keys with a small soft paintbrush.

3 If the keyboard is very dusty, use canned air to clear dust from around the keys.

To clean the mouse

1 Remove the track ball cover.

2 Remove the track ball.

3 Clean inside the mouse with a cotton swab dampened with alcohol.

4 Replace the track ball and cover.

Caring for books

The best way to keep books at their best is to read them, but there are also several other things you can do to ensure they remain in good condition.

- Regularly open books to help reduce dampness as well as prevent dust from setting too deep.

- Store books in glass-fronted cabinets to protect them from dust and sunlight, ideally at a temperature of around 15°C (59°F), but make sure there is adequate ventilation.

- Store heavy books flat to prevent the pages tearing away from the spine, and use book ends to stop books slumping against each other and becoming damaged.

- Dust books once a year by brushing the page edges with a thick make-up brush while the book is closed.

Putting up a simple shelf

Here is a simple method to put up some quick shelving.

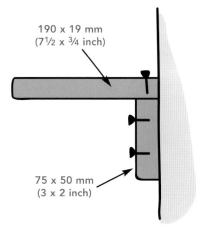

190 x 19 mm
(7½ x ¾ inch)

75 x 50 mm
(3 x 2 inch)

1 Simply screw or nail a piece of 75- x 50-mm (3- x 2-inch) timber exactly level to the wall, the same length as the shelf.

2 Make sure it's solid, then screw down into the top of your 75- x 50-mm (3- x 2-inch) a piece of 190- x 19-mm (7½- x ¾-inch) timber to act as the shelf. If you need lots of shelving, buy a sheet of plywood and get the timber yard to cut it down to 200-mm (8-inch) strips and then cut it yourself to suit your shelving.

Caring for photographs

Your photographs will last much longer if you look after them properly.

- Store treasured photographs in good-quality paper albums interleaved with acid-free paper.

- Store photographs in a cool, dark, dry place, such as under the bed.

- Use photo corners rather than glue to secure photos in place.

- Store negatives and old prints out of sunlight, at an even temperature. Place them in polyester covers to prevent the surfaces sticking together and to avoid bleaching of colours.

Caring for pictures

Calculated neglect is the best treatment for paintings. They need a little of the right attention but nothing too harsh. Keep paintings away from humid places or rooms that may vary abruptly in temperature. Bathrooms and kitchens, attics and basements, then, are usually out of bounds. Also, don't hang pictures near windows, where rain or sun could damage them, or near smoky candles.

Seek specialist attention for very valuable artwork. For other less expensive or cherished pieces you can apply some home treatment.

- To clean unpainted wooden frames use a soft cloth dipped in linseed oil.

- Clean painted frames with a cloth that has been dampened with mild soap solution.

- To remove discolouration from gilt frames, rub with a piece of lemon, sponge with a solution of 1 teaspoon bicarbonate of soda in 2 cups warm water, then polish with chamois leather.

- Dust picture glass with a soft cloth. To remove marks, use a little methylated spirits (denatured alcohol) or other glass cleaner — just enough to make the cloth damp — on a soft cloth. Never spray the glass with a liquid as some may seep behind the glass and come into contact with the painting.

- Never touch paintings that are not behind glass as skin oils can cause damage over time. Just gently dust these paintings with extreme care once a year. Use a fine soft brush and work from top to bottom.

Hanging a picture

BRICK WALL

For a small picture you'll need an impact drill — one with a hammer action on it so it can drill through bricks.

1 Using a 6-mm (¼-inch) masonry drill bit, drill a hole about 50 mm (2 inches) deep into your brickwork.

2 Wall plugs are available at every hardware store. They're colour coded according to their size, so 6 mm (¼ inch) is a green plug. Tap the green plug into your hole until it's flush with the wall.

3 Each plug suits a certain screw size — just check the packet. Once you have the right screw, about 50 mm (2 inches) long and 6 gauge, screw it in. Leave about 10 mm (½ inch) sticking out of the plug and hang your picture.

For larger pictures you can go up through the various sizes of plugs and screws, or buy a Dynabolt with a cup hook. It has the same principle as the plug and screw. There are various sizes of Dynabolt available, depending on the size of your painting.

1 Drill the hole to suit the size of the Dynabolt.

2 Tap the bolt straight in the hole and tighten it. The outside sleeve on the Dynabolt spreads and the bolt tightens on itself.

TIMBER WALL

It's always a good idea to find the structural timber in the wall. Allow the thickness of the lining board (usually either 6 mm or ¼ inch for fibro or 10 mm or ½ inch for gyprock), about 30 mm (1¼ inch) penetration into the stud work and 10 mm (½ inch) proud to hang the picture.

You cannot put a screw straight into plasterboard as it isn't strong enough. You must find the solid timber behind for strength. If that's impossible, there are a few things available on the market for going into plasterboard. Try a wall mate or a toggle.

If you're hanging a very heavy picture onto a plasterboard wall, try to find a stud. Knock along the wall with your knuckle, listening for a change in tone. The hollow-sounding bits don't have a stud behind them, so listen for a 'solid' sound.

Flowers in the house

Flowers add colour and grace to any room of your home, not just the living room. A few tricks can make their beauty last longer. To prolong the life of cut flowers, follow these tips:

- If cutting flowers from the garden, cut on a cloudy day or early in the morning to minimize moisture loss. Make clean cuts with pruning shears or a sharp knife.

TO REVIVE CUT FLOWERS

Plunge the stems into boiling water. By the time the water is cool, the flowers will have revived. Cut off the ends of the stems and place the flowers in fresh cold water.

- Plunge the stems into a bucket of tepid water as soon as you have cut them.
- Encourage flowers to absorb water by cutting stems every few days.
- When recutting green stems, cut a 5-cm (2-inch) slit up the stem from the base, then cut the bottom of the stem at a 45-degree angle.
- Cut stems under water to prevent air bubbles entering the stems.
- Let cut flowers stand in deep water for several hours before arranging them.
- On woody plants, scrape away the bark on the lower 5 cm (2 inches) of the stem, then slit it and recut.
- Remove lower leaves on stems as when they are submerged, they rot, producing gas that can hasten wilting.
- Trim buds that will not blossom to allow more water to go to flowers.
- If you are arranging tulips, add a few drops of vodka to the water to keep the stems standing straight.

Preserving flowers

Preserve flowers by adding 2 teaspoons medicinal mouthwash to every 4 litres (140 fl oz) water, although you could also try aspirin or a little sugar. Alternatively, the acid in a clear soft drink also works — add 1 can soft drink to every 4 litres (140 fl oz) water.

Plant life

Fungus on house plants is unhealthy for you as well as the plant. First, trim badly affected leaves and discard them. Make up a spray using 1 tablespoon bicarbonate of soda to every 4 litres (140 fl oz) water. Repeat every few days until there is no sign of the fungus.

Drying flowers

You can save the blooms from the garden or from a bouquet, dry them and transform them into scented gifts or decorations to fill the house with perfume and colour all year round.

Air drying — hanging

Hanging flowers in bunches and leaving them to dry naturally is one of the easiest drying techniques. Flowers such as roses are especially suited to this particular technique.

1 Pick the flowers on a sunny day. Ideally, the flowers should be picked at about mid morning — by this time the dew has dried and the flowers have not been exposed to the heat of the midday sun.

2 Remove the excess foliage from the stems. If you want to dry the leaves as well, leave a few on the stems and remove them after the flowers have dried. If drying roses, remove the thorns to make handling easier.

3 Gather the flowers into small bunches — 8 to 10 flowers in each bunch. Any more and the flowers will take too long to dry.

4 Arrange the flowers so that the flower heads are at different levels. This encourages air circulation around the stems and flower heads, and reduces the risk of the stems becoming mouldy. Trim the bottom of the flowers with florist's scissors.

5 Fasten the bunches together firmly using elastic bands or thin strips of pantihose (tights). As the stems dry they will shrink slightly — the elastic will adjust as the stems shrink and will keep the flowers in place.

6 Tie a piece of string around the elastic band and hang upside down to dry in a garage or airing cupboard, out of direct sunlight. Hanging the plants in a dark place will help them to retain their colour as they dry. Leave space between the bunches to allow air to circulate freely.

7 It will take from 1 to 4 weeks for the flowers to dry, depending on the type of flower, the weather and the amount of moisture in the leaves. When completely dry, the flowers should feel slightly crisp and the leaves should be dry and brittle.

Air drying — upright

This method is suited to flowers with woody stems such as eucalypts, hydrangeas, mimosa and delphinium, or tall grasses and seed heads.

1 Fill the bottom of a vase or container with about 5 cm (2 inches) of water and place the flowers or grasses standing upright in the water. To support the heads of larger flowers and to prevent them from becoming damaged, place chicken wire over the top of the container and thread the stems through the wire.

2 Place the container in a warm area, but not in direct sunlight. The water will evaporate after being absorbed by the plant, and the flower will dry slowly. The vase may need to be topped up with water.

Air drying — flat

This technique is suitable for delicate plant materials, or if you want to dry flower petals for use in pot-pourri. Petals from cornflowers, roses, larkspur and peonies, and flower heads, such as zinnias, carnations and roses, are all suitable.

1 Line a tea tray or flat basket with a piece of newspaper or paper towel and position the petals or flower heads on top. If drying flower heads, place them face up and space them so they are not touching one another. Petals should be spread out on the tray in a single layer.

2 Place the tray in an area where there is plenty of dry air circulating.

3 Check the plant materials daily and turn them over. Depending on the flower, drying time may vary from a few days to a week. When the flower is dry it should feel crisp to touch.

4 Place the dried materials in airtight containers and store in a dark place.

Oven drying

1 Place the petals or flowers on an oven-proof tray, ensuring the petals do not overlap.

2 Set the oven to the lowest setting and place the tray in the oven, leaving the door slightly ajar.

3 Check the flowers regularly. Depending on the thickness of the flowers you are drying, the process can take anywhere from a few minutes to several hours.

kitchen

The kitchen is the hub of the house. It is also the room where you prepare, and possibly eat, your meals, so it needs to be scrupulously clean at all times. This chapter provides hundreds of hints designed to help you get kitchen cleaning down to a fine art. There are tips for cleaning silver and other metals, repairing items around the kitchen, as well as information on buying and storing foods, freezing and microwaving, storing wine, measurement conversions and cooking terminology.

The ideal kitchen

The clever kitchen is kept clean — with low-toxic cleaners — and well ventilated to reduce bacteria. It uses energy-efficient appliances and has water-saving features.

- **Ventilation** The clever kitchen should be well ventilated to counteract the mould-encouraging effect of steam and to dissipate combustion by-products — both produced by cooking. This helps make the kitchen a healthier place for all household members, especially those who may be prone to mould- and mildew-induced allergies, or to respiratory allergies and irritations that are made worse by pollutant gases. Managing moisture in the kitchen has a knock-on effect throughout the house: keep the door closed when it's hot and steamy.

- **Energy-efficient appliances** The clever kitchen uses a top-rating, energy-efficient fridge, freezer and stove which are ideally run on a combination of solar power and natural gas back-up.

- **Tap water** This is rainwater which is hygienically collected and regularly tested to check it conforms to drinking water standards.

- **Waste water** This passes into the household water recycling system, which has good-quality filter systems. Once treated, this water is used on the garden, to flush the household toilets as well as to wash clothes.

- **Detergent** Dishwashing liquids and other cleaners are phosphate-free and low in toxic additives.

- **Recycling corner** All items recycled by the local authority — glass, paper, steel, plastic, aluminium — are stored for recycling and regular pick-up. Other items, such as batteries and tyres, are periodically removed to a local recycling depot. Some items are kept for recycling in the house.

- **Biodegradable scraps** All compost items are placed in a mini kitchen bin and regularly taken out to the compost heap.

- **Safety** Dangerous items such as sharp knives and toxic chemicals are kept out of reach.

- **Kitchen pests** These are controlled with natural methods.

Storing equipment

- Spatulas, wooden spoons and light wooden utensils can easily be kept upright in a glass, ceramic or metal container positioned on a worktop.

- Rails or rods and butcher's hooks are popular hanging options. You can use a wooden pole in a country or traditionally decorated kitchen, or steel in a more contemporary one. Butcher's hooks are S-shaped, made of steel and come in two sizes — the larger size is big enough to support pots and pans whereas the smaller size is ideal for hanging spoons, spatulas and whisks from. When hanging heavier items ensure the rail is strong enough to support the weight. If you use a long rail that is holding heavy weights then you may need to put a couple of extra support brackets, fixed to the wall or ceiling, along the rail. If you want an alternative to a rail then you can use a chain. This chain should be made of a strong metal with good-sized links. The chain can be hung horizontally between two points or cut in varying lengths that are individually hung and allowed to fall vertically.

- Storage jars need not always be shut away in a cupboard. Think about displaying them on a shelf to add a decorative feature and also to allow easy access to the items stored within them, such as tea, coffee and sugar. Give such jars a sense of unity by choosing a matching set, such as steel and glass or white ceramic containers. Glass containers are extremely good for display as they show the contents from top to bottom.

- Plate racks can be fitted inside a cupboard or on the wall over the work surface. These enable you to slot washed, flat tableware in between the sections in order to leave them there to dry.

Displaying kitchen equipment

Although the clean worktop approach is advocated in modern kitchens, a few useful pieces of equipment can be left on show to soften the edges and provide the feeling of a lived-in space.

- Salt and pepper mills are often placed on an open shelf so that they are easily accessible because they are in constant use. Mills come in a variety of shapes and sizes and materials but a matching pair of chrome, glass or wood pieces will look very appealing in any kitchen. Choose a pair that will go with your overall colour scheme.

- Classic pieces of equipment such as a designer juice squeezer, a cafetière or French coffee percolator are common show pieces. A neat espresso coffee maker and a kettle are also fashionable kitchen equipment. The rule with this sort of accessory is that it should be both useful and beautiful. If you are leaving it on display then make sure that you choose the nicest shape, the best finish and also the one that has the most interesting lines, because it will become part of the look of the kitchen.

Kitchen recycling

It's hard to avoid all the packaging that seems to come home with the shopping, but a great deal of it can be creatively recycled.

- Jars can be used as airtight containers for spices and grains.

- Plastic shopping bags can be reused for lining bins, especially bathroom ones, wrapping around disposable nappies, holding wet swimming gear — and shopping.

- Young children can build a play supermarket with cereal packets, toothpaste and tea boxes, egg cartons and empty plastic bottles.

- Collect bottle corks to make a cork board. Cut each cork in half lengthways and stick the halves with strong glue to a piece of board. Corks also make good kindling for fires, but take care not to use plastic ones.

THE FRUIT BOWL

Fresh fruit and vegetables can bring a pleasant splash of colour to a kitchen and will also be a constantly changing embellishment as you replace what you have eaten from the display.

To display fruit and vegetables well, look at open-weave metal baskets, which allow the fruit to show through and also breathe, and glass bowl containers. The disadvantage with glass bowls is that they restrict the airflow to the lower fruits, which means that they will ripen and rot much more quickly. Make sure that you use fruit and vegetables within a few days, before they start to go wrinkled or mouldy.

- Cardboard boxes can be called into service as storage boxes. Turn the flaps inside the box and fix them down with sticky tape for extra strength. Decorate the box by covering it in wrapping paper. They are also welcome — if temporary — toys for children to make into houses, boats and rockets.

- Tea leaves, onion skins and turmeric all make safe natural dyes for crafts.

- Egg cartons are ideal seed-propagation trays. The whole cup can be planted in the garden at the appropriate time — just cut out the bottom.

Energy-saving tips

There are many ways to use less energy when cooking and storing food, and clearing up afterwards. It needn't be harder or take more time.

- Choose a dishwasher that allows you to eliminate the heated drying cycle and dry by air instead, or turn your machine off before that phase.

- Save water by using the dishwasher's rinse and hold function instead of rinsing dishes before you load them into the machine.

- Wash only full loads in the dishwasher.

- Run the dishwasher at its lower temperature settings.

- Use a dishwasher detergent with low environmental impact. Alternatively, replace up to 50 per cent of a standard detergent with washing soda.

- Where appropriate, use small appliances, such as pressure cookers, toasters and electric kettles.

- Match the size of pots to the size of a hot plate or burner — turn down the burner if flames are lapping up the side of the pan.

- Use the minimum amount of water when boiling or steaming.

- If possible, cook more than one item in the oven simultaneously.

- Leave the oven door shut. When you open the oven door the temperature can drop by as much as 15°C (59°F). It takes more energy to restore the correct temperature.

- Microwave ovens use less energy than conventional ovens. Fan-forced ovens use less than conventional ones, but more than microwave ovens.

- Locate fridges in cool spots — not in the sun, nor next to the oven.

- Ensure good circulation around the coils and dust them regularly.

- Keep the fridge defrosted to enable maximum efficiency.

- Keep the fridge door seals clean and in good condition. (To test your seal, try closing the door on a sheet of paper. If you can pull it out easily, the seal is not working properly.)

- Run the fridge between 3°C and 5°C (37.4°F and 41°F). Freezers should run at a temperature of between −15°C and −18°C (5°F and 0.4°F). Every degree lower costs 5 per cent more in running costs and greenhouse gas pollution.

- Shut that door! Be quick when you open the fridge door as the longer it is open, the more it will warm up.

- Cut down the chances of ice forming inside the fridge by covering all containers containing liquids.

MAKE CLEANING EASIER

■ Reduce the likelihood of spills by covering food while cooking in the microwave.

■ Use splatter guards on hot frying pans.

■ Don't overfill saucepans.

Cleaning and maintenance

Even if you don't care for cleaning any other part of the house, you should always keep the kitchen spotless and follow the rules of hygiene when storing and preparing food.

Work surfaces

The rule with cleaning the kitchen is to clean as you go — before food preparation and afterwards. Most surfaces can be cleaned with a cloth dipped in mild detergent and hot water. These surfaces include Corian, laminate, marble, slate and tiles. Some may be lightly scoured, while others may need oil.

- **Corian** It's a good idea to use a gentle scourer for stains on Corian, which is a blend of natural materials and pure acrylic polymer. Treat stubborn ones with very fine abrasive paper, then polish with a soft cloth.

- **Granite** Wipe regularly with a hot cloth. Clean greasy marks with a few drops of household ammonia in water.

- **Laminate** Use a few drops of eucalyptus oil to disinfect. For tough marks, use neat detergent, leave for a few minutes then rinse. Do not scour. Take care with hot saucepans. Although laminate can take heat from pans and cooking utensils, it will become damaged if they are left to stand.

- **Slate** To shine, wipe with a few drops of lemon oil then polish with a soft dry cloth.

- **Tiles** To remove stains, try rubbing on salt with a cut lemon.

- **Sealed wood** Pots and pans should go on a tile or board to prevent burns to the bench surface.

- **Unsealed wood** Rub with boiled linseed oil and wipe excess off with a soft cloth. Try salt and lemon on stains and scorch marks.

Chopping boards

- **Plastic** Scrub with a small brush with hot water and detergent. Most are also fine in the dishwasher. To kill bacteria, wipe over with a mild solution of household bleach.

- **Wood** Rub with a little vegetable oil to protect from splitting and warping. Scrub well with a stiff-bristled brush and hot water to remove stains. Clear food odours by rubbing with salt — a natural disinfectant — and cut lemon. Store where plenty of air can circulate.

CHOPPING BOARD HYGIENE
The hygienic kitchen needs two chopping boards — one for vegetables, one for meat. If chopping raw and cooked meat, scrub the board well after chopping the raw meat.

Repairing chipped edges on laminate work surface

1 If the edge has chipped, glue the broken piece of laminate back in position, if possible, using neat PVA.

2 Use masking tape to hold the section securely in position while the glue dries.

Reparing scratches on laminate work surface

To deal with surface scratches, simply dust and clean the area then paint along the groove with a fine artist's brush using an oil-based enamel paint. Try and match the worktop colour as closely as possible. For a patterned worktop it is best to choose one of the darkest colours in its design. Wipe away any excess.

Fixing drawer fronts

Drawer fronts often become loose, as the effectiveness of the screw fixings lessens with constant use.

1 To remedy this problem, simply unscrew the drawer front and apply a generous amount of wood glue or PVA to the back face.

2 Screw the front back onto the drawer carcass. It is important for the back face of the drawer front and the front face of the carcass to be pressed together very tightly, in order to ensure proper adhesion. You may therefore need to attach some clamps to hold the front firmly in position. Although the screw fixings for the drawer front will remain slightly loose, the combined effect of the glue and screws will hold the drawer front back in the desired position.

Fixing drawer handles

The daily opening and closing of drawers will take its toll on the screw fixings for handles, which may become loose or fall off completely. For obvious aesthetic reasons it will not be possible to reposition the handle and make new fixings altogether.

1 To repair a loosened handle, therefore, you will need to unscrew it and apply a small amount of resin to the thread of the fixing bolt.

2 Screw the handle back in position using washers to help spread the force put on the handle when the drawer is opened. This technique can also be applied to door handles and handles with only one fixing point.

Repairing drawer runners

Drawer runners in old pieces of furniture are often worn away so that the drawers are difficult to pull out and push in. They are not very difficult to repair.

1 Use a chisel to pare away the worn timber of the runner until the runner is once again level.

2 Nail or glue a thin strip of hardwood to the runner to build it back to the required thickness.

Natural kitchen cleaner recipes

Why use dangerous chemicals when almost everything you need to keep your kitchen clean — and much less toxic — is probably in your store cupboard!

THE RAW INGREDIENTS

Here's a list of basic ingredients for making all the cleaners you need.

- Bicarbonate of soda
- Ammonia
- Bleach
- White vinegar
- Washing soda
- Laundry detergent
- Washing up liquid

All-purpose cleaner 1

INGREDIENTS

2 heaped tablespoons bicarbonate of soda

1 tablespoon white vinegar

METHOD

Mix the bicarbonate of soda and white vinegar together and store the cleaner in an airtight container.

All-purpose cleaner 2

This recipe makes a mild cleaner and deodorizer suitable for light soiling on the fridge, oven and any other surfaces.

INGREDIENTS

4 tablespoons bicarbonate of soda

1.5 litres (52 fl oz/6 cups) warm water

METHOD

Mix the ingredients together. Wipe surfaces with a soft cloth dipped in the solution. Rinse with clean water.

Strong all-purpose cleaner 1

This cleaner can be used in kitchens and bathrooms, on floors, tiles, cupboards, appliances, ovens and so on, but not on fibreglass or aluminium.

INGREDIENTS

125 ml (4 fl oz/$\frac{1}{2}$ cup) washing soda

4.5 litres (156 fl oz/18 cups) warm water

METHOD

Mix the ingredients together.

Strong all-purpose cleaner 2

This is a good all-round cleaner for many surfaces and materials including kitchen appliances, glass and silver. It will also strip floor wax and dissolve resinous matter.

INGREDIENTS

4 litres (140 fl oz/16 cups) hot water

100 ml (3$\frac{1}{2}$ fl oz) household ammonia

100 ml (3$\frac{1}{2}$ fl oz) white vinegar

200 g (7 oz) bicarbonate of soda

METHOD

Mix the ingredients together and store in a tightly sealed bottle.

Mild abrasive cleaner

Use this cleaner on plastic and on painted walls.

INGREDIENTS

Few drops of water

Bicarbonate of soda

METHOD

Add a few drops of water to bicarbonate of soda to form a paste. Apply it with a stiff-bristled brush on hard surfaces, and with an old toothbrush between tiles.

Scouring cleaner 1

INGREDIENTS

1 teaspoon borax

2 tablespoons white vinegar

500 ml (17 fl oz/2 cups) hot water

METHOD

Combine the ingredients together and pour the mixture into a spray bottle.

Scouring cleaner 2

INGREDIENTS

½ cup bicarbonate of soda

3 tablespoons sodium perborate

METHOD

Mix the bicarbonate of soda with the sodium perborate. Use a wet sponge to rub the mixture onto areas that need whitening. Leave for 10–15 minutes before rinsing.

Disinfectant 1

This disinfectant can be used in the kitchen, bathroom and around the house on various surfaces, including marble, plastic, fibreglass, fridges, nursery furniture such as cots and high chairs, plastic mattress covers and ceramic tiles (although you should test first on dark colours or coloured grout).

INGREDIENTS

185 ml (6 fl oz/¾ cup) bleach

1.5 litres (52 fl oz/6 cups) warm water

1 tablespoon powdered laundry detergent

METHOD

Mix the ingredients together. Wash the surface and keep it wet for 5 minutes before rinsing and allowing it to dry.

Disinfectant 2

INGREDIENTS

1 teaspoon borax

2 tablespoons distilled white vinegar

60 ml (2 fl oz/¼ cup) liquid soap

500 ml (17 fl oz/2 cups) hot water

METHOD

Mix the ingredients together. Use this disinfectant in the same way as 'Disinfectant 1' above, or store it in a spray bottle and spray it on.

Disinfectant 3

Use this disinfectant for hairbrushes and combs, mopping vinyl, and sanitizing and deodorizing garbage bins.

INGREDIENTS

185 ml (6 fl oz/¾ cup) bleach

1.5 litres (52 fl oz/6 cups) water

METHOD

Mix the ingredients together. Keep the surfaces wet for 5 minutes, rinse and allow to dry.

Disinfectant 4

INGREDIENTS

2 teaspoons borax

4 tablespoons white vinegar

750 ml (26 fl oz/3 cups) hot water

METHOD

Mix together all the ingredients. Pour the mixture into a spray bottle. For greater cleaning power, add ¼ teaspoon liquid soap.

All-purpose spray cleaner

This all-purpose cleaner is suitable for the kitchen and bathroom.

INGREDIENTS

4 litres (140 fl oz/16 cups) hot water

2 tablespoons cloudy ammonia

125 ml (4 fl oz/½ cup) white vinegar

2 tablespoons bicarbonate of soda

2 drops lavender or lemon oil

2 tablespoons basic household soap cleaner

METHOD

In a bucket, mix all the ingredients into the water. Allow to cool, then fill spray bottles.

Wall and paint cleaner

INGREDIENTS

1 litre (35 fl oz/4 cups) hot water

60 ml (2 fl oz/¼ cup) washing soda crystals

4 litres (140 fl oz/16 cups) cold water

125 ml (4 fl oz/½ cup) cloudy ammonia

125 ml (4 fl oz/½ cup) white vinegar

METHOD

Mix the hot water and washing soda crystals together in a bucket. Add the cold water, then the cloudy ammonia and the white vinegar.

Disinfecting floor cleaner

INGREDIENTS

½ cup borax

3 litres (104 fl oz/12 cups) hot water

METHOD

Mix the borax and hot water together. Use the cleaner with a cloth or mop as usual.

KITCHEN HANDS

To remove fruit stains from your hands, mix a little caster sugar into some olive oil to make a paste. Rub this well into the skin, leave for a few minutes then wash your hands in warm soapy water. Stubborn stains may require three goes. To remove the smell of onions from your hands, rub well with celery or parsley.

The kitchen sink

Although these days many households have a dishwasher, the sink is still an essential part of the kitchen. Wipe the sink down each time you wash up, and scrub it at least weekly. If it needs a little more attention, check the following useful tips.

- **Acrylic** Remove water marks with white vinegar. Never use an abrasive cleaner such as an abrasive cleansing cream or a scourer on acrylic, as you will risk scratching the surface. Remove scratches with metal polish.

- **Corian** Clean as for a Corian work surface (see page 97). To restore colour to a stained sink, fill the sink with a solution of 1 part household bleach to 4 parts water. Leave for half an hour, then drain and rinse.

- **Enamel** Do not use bleach or scourers on enamel. Remove stains with borax and a cut lemon or a paste of bicarbonate of soda and hydrogen peroxide (a gentle bleach). Start with bicarbonate of soda and add just enough hydrogen peroxide to make a paste. Rub, allow to dry, then rinse off.

KITCHEN SPONGES

To freshen and revitalize kitchen sponges and cloths, dissolve a generous handful of salt and 1 tablespoon of washing soda in 4 cups of warm water. Dunk the cloths, leave for a couple of minutes, rinse in cold water and allow to dry.

- **Stainless steel** To avoid scratches, don't use abrasive cleaners or scourers. Use neat detergent on stains. For a shiny look, polish with methylated spirits (denatured alcohol) and a dry cloth.

Keeping the drain clear

A little attention now and then can prevent serious blockages developing.

- **Selective disposal** The first step in trying to keep drains clear is to put as little as possible down the drain in the first place. Catch food debris and prevent it clogging the drain pipes by using a sink strainer before disposing of the scraps in the compost. Use the compost bin for biodegradable matter, including tea leaves and coffee grounds, and scrape fat and oil into the garbage rather than wash up dishes and pans caked with fat.

- **Boiling water** Pour boiling water down the kitchen sink to melt grease and wash it away.

- **Drain cleaners** Keep the kitchen drain clear by regularly using a drain cleaner. It's much less time-consuming than clearing an already blocked drain. Commercial drain cleaners often use sodium hydroxide and aluminium. These rely on bubbling from aluminium and heat formed when the sodium hydroxide dissolves, to agitate and melt grease. Or try one of the home remedies listed on page 107.

Caring for taps

To remove caked dirt from kitchen taps, use a toothbrush dipped in detergent or bicarbonate of soda. Most taps can be washed in a hot detergent solution or a solution of bicarbonate of soda.

- **Brass and copper** Wipe a lacquered finish on brass or copper taps with a damp cloth. Use metal polish on unlacquered surfaces. To remove verdigris or other tarnishes, rub gently with a paste of salt and lemon juice. Alternatively, wipe with household ammonia, rinse and dry with a soft cloth.

- **Chrome** Polish chrome taps with a cloth soaked in white vinegar or a weak solution of household ammonia in water.

UNBLOCKING THE DRAIN — THE NATURAL WAY

When the water won't drain and you are faced with a sink full of water, try one of these natural drain cleaners, then use a plunger. Place the plunger tightly over the drain hole, push down then pull up rapidly, keeping the plunger over the hole. If your seal is tight, the air and water inside the pipe is forced back and forth, with any luck sloshing and sucking the blockage away. If you are unsuccessful, try a different drain cleaner and leave overnight.

■ Sodium bicarbonate and vinegar

Ingredients

½–1 cup sodium bicarbonate
250 ml (9 fl oz/1 cup) white vinegar

Method

Pour the sodium bicarbonate down the drain, then slowly pour in the white vinegar. The sizzling sound is the reaction between the two. Follow with water and repeat the whole process if necessary.

■ Ammonia in boiling water

Ingredients

2 teaspoons household ammonia
Kettle of boiling water

Method

For moderate blocks, try household ammonia chased with a kettle of boiling water. Then use the plunger to loosen the blockage.

■ Washing soda and boiling water

Ingredients

2 cups washing soda crystals
Kettle of boiling water

Method

Pile the washing soda at the opening of the drain then slowly pour on a kettle of boiling water.

The stove

Cleaning a dirt-encrusted stove once in a while is a very time-consuming and labour-intensive job. It's certainly one of those jobs where a little prevention is much better than hours of unpleasant cure, so try to get in the habit of cleaning as you go and encourage anyone else who uses the stove to do the same thing.

- **The stove top** Every time you use the stove top, wipe it with hot water to prevent a build-up of spillages. Avoid abrasive cleaners on stainless steel and enamel tops. For encrusted stains, try a poultice made from a cloth soaked in a cleaning solution, leave for a few hours then wipe away. Alternatively, apply a caustic cleaner with a toothbrush, leave for a few hours, then scrub the mixture off with hot water.

- **The grill (broiler) pan** It's best to wash the grill pan in hot water and detergent after each use. But if your domestic routine slips up and you find yourself with a build-up of grease, scrape out the solids with a spatula, wipe the pan with balls of newspaper, then wash it.

- **The oven** Commercial oven cleaners contain highly caustic, unpleasant substances. To avoid having to use these, don't let the

OVEN CLEANERS

When you do have to clean the oven, try one of these alternatives to strong commercial cleaners.

Preheat the oven to warm, or proceed immediately after cooking in the oven. Place 125 ml (4 fl oz/½ cup) of cloudy ammonia inside, shut the door and switch off the oven. Leave overnight if possible, or for at least a few hours. Wipe thoroughly with hot water and detergent.

Wet the surface and sprinkle it with bicarbonate of soda. Rub with fine steel wool then wipe off the residue with a damp cloth. Repeat if necessary. Rinse well and dry.

To clean very dirty shelves, soak them in a mixture of 1 part washing soda to 4 parts hot water. If the shelves are too large to submerge fully in the sink, turn them around every 20 minutes, or use the bath or laundry sink.

oven get too dirty before getting round to cleaning it. Wipe the surfaces with a hot, damp cloth after each use and clean up spills on the oven floor.

Large kitchen appliances

Most kitchen appliances can be wiped and washed with hot water and detergent or another general purpose cleanser of your choice, such as bicarbonate of soda mixed with water, which is mild, non-toxic and environmentally friendly. Here are some specific tips:

- **Microwaves** For stubborn stains, place a bowl of hot water in the microwave and switch on to High (100%) for 5 minutes. Allow to stand for a few minutes and remove. Wipe inside with a soft cloth.

- **Dishwasher** Clean the filters and seals on your dishwasher regularly. To restore a dull interior, run the machine empty on a short cycle with 500 ml (17 fl oz/2 cups) vinegar in the detergent receptacle.

- **Fridge** Use a solution of 1 part bicarbonate of soda to 7 parts water to wipe down the inside of the fridge. Wash any removable parts in hot water and detergent. To prevent mould from forming on the door seals, wipe over them with white vinegar. If you can reach them, vacuum the coils behind the fridge using your vacuum cleaner's brush attachment. To absorb odours, place a small, open bowl of bicarbonate of soda on one of the shelves. Change it regularly.

SWEET AND FRESH
To leave the fridge smelling fresh, wipe over the inside with a damp cloth and a few drops of vanilla essence.

Small appliances

Here is some general advice on caring for and cleaning small kitchen appliances. (Always remember to turn off the power and remove the plug from the socket before cleaning any electrical item, and also be sure to check the manufacturer's instructions on cleaning.)

- Wipe over chrome appliances with a paste made from bicarbonate of soda and water.

- Always wipe over an appliance with a damp cloth immediately after using it.

- Once washable parts, such as a processor bowl, are disassembled, rinse them in hot water, removing food debris with a soft brush.

- To clean your can opener, use a toothbrush and warm water with detergent in it. After drying, rub a little cooking oil over the teeth.

- Do not immerse electrical components in water unless advised to by the manufacturer.

- Dry each part carefully before storing.

MOULD-FREE
To prevent mould growing when your fridge and freezer are empty and switched off for more than a few days, wipe the inside with vinegar and leave the doors propped open.

Washing up

Washing up isn't a hi-tech task but it's one that takes up a lot of time — you've no sooner finished one lot than it's time to do another.

Washing cutlery

- **Cutlery stains** Dissolve a little salt in lemon juice. Dip a soft cloth into the solution and rub the cutlery. Rinse in warm water and rub with a chamois.

- **Bone and wood handles** Never leave handles of ivory, wood, horn or bone lying in the water. Stand the metal parts in a jar of hot washing up water, wipe the handles with a hot damp cloth and dry.

- **Silver and silver plate** Wash silver cutlery as soon as possible: some foods leave stains that are hard to remove the longer you leave them.

NATURAL WAYS TO DE-SCALE YOUR KETTLE

Cover the element with vinegar then top up with water. Bring to the boil and leave overnight, preferably for about 12 hours. Pour the liquid away.

Fill the kettle with water and place it in the fridge overnight. The build-up comes loose in the cold. Next, boil the water; the lime will dissolve in it and can be poured away.

- **Stainless steel** Do not use steel wool. Rinse soon after using as acidic or salty foods may cause pit marks.

- **Bronze** Thai bronze cutlery can be treated like stainless steel. Remove green spots by rubbing with a soft cloth dipped in turpentine, then wash.

Basic dishwashing liquid

Use 1 teaspoon to 5 litres (175 fl oz/20 cups) water when washing up, or use 250 ml (9 fl oz/1 cup) per load in a dishwasher. (This won't remove coffee and tea stains.)

INGREDIENTS

50 g (1¾ oz) pure soap

125 ml (4 fl oz/½ cup) washing soda crystals

125 ml (4 fl oz/½ cup) white vinegar

1½ teaspoons eucalyptus oil or tea-tree oil

Few drops lemon or lavender pure essential oil for fragrance

5 litres (175 fl oz/20 cups) cold water

4.5 litres (158 fl oz/18 cups) hot water

METHOD

1 Grate the soap into a large saucepan and cover with 1 litre (35 fl oz/4 cups) of the cold water. Bring to the boil, add the washing soda and stir until it is completely dissolved.

2 Stir in the eucalyptus oil, vinegar and essential oil.

3 Pour into a bucket, add the hot water then stir in the remaining cold water.

4 When cool, transfer to smaller containers and label.

The idiot's guide to washing up

The right tools ease the burden of the daily drudgery of washing up. If you don't have a dishwasher, it's helpful to have plate racks, draining board, bottle brushes, hand mop, wire brush, plastic and metal scouring pads — and lots of clean tea towels.

- Stack dishes and pans in like piles — plates in one pile, glasses grouped together, pans and sticky utensils in another.

- Scrape all food scraps into the compost bin (using a spatula on surfaces that might be damaged by scratching).

- Start with very hot water and a squeeze of washing up liquid or cleaning aid of your choice. A bowl inside the sink means you can still tip liquids into the sink while washing up. It's kinder on crockery and glass at the same time.

- Wash glasses first and rinse before resting them on a draining rack to dry.

- Rinsing can be in a second sink, if you have one, under a slow-running tap (turn it off when you tackle dirty saucepans or shift a new stack into the bowl) or a plastic bowl or bucket placed on a stool near the sink.

- The rest of the washing up should be in order of cleanliness: cleanest first, dirtiest last.

- Change the water when it gets dirtier than the next bowl of dishes!

LESS WASHING UP
You can cut down on the volume of messy washing up by taking just a few precautionary measures.
- Put a sheet of paper towel on the turntable in the microwave. It will catch spills.
- Put foil inside the grill (broiler) pan.
- When reheating food, especially for solo diners, consider using a single bowl in the microwave rather than a saucepan and a bowl.

Installing a dishwasher

If you have all the required fittings, you can install a dishwasher yourself. If not, a plumber is required.

1 The water intake is the same as the one on a washing machine. Just screw that onto the tap fitting under the sink.

2 Next attach the dishwasher waste. There should be a dishwasher waste on your kitchen sink trap. If you haven't got one you'll need a new trap. It's best to get a plumber to do this.

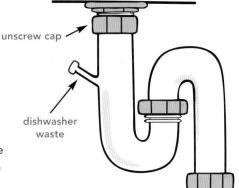

unscrew cap

dishwasher
waste

3 The most important thing to check is that the dishwasher waste on the trap has been drilled out. When the traps are new they are sealed. A 10 mm (½ in) hole is enough.

4 Finally, place the dishwasher waste on with a hose clamp, and then tighten it up with a screwdriver.

Specific cleaning methods

Here are a few tried and true tips, both old and new, to keep everything in your kitchen sparkling clean.

Lemon fresh

To wash and deodorize the fridge, bin or kitchen compost container, use a solution of 1 teaspoon lemon juice to 4 cups water.

Tarnished silver cutlery

A quick fix for tarnished cutlery is to place a piece of aluminium foil into a plastic bucket and sprinkle over 3 tablespoons bicarbonate of soda. Lay the silver on top. Cover with hot water. Leave until bubbles stop, rinse and polish with a dry, soft cloth.

For sparkling crystal

Dip crystal in a solution of 1 part vinegar to 3 parts water. Polish with a dry, lint-free cloth.

Washing glass

Wash glass water bottles and flower vases with 1 tablespoon vinegar and 1 tablespoon salt in warm water. Allow to stand for several hours and shake occasionally.

Wash very dirty cut glass in warm soapy water to which a few drops of ammonia have been added, and scrub gently with a small brush. (Do not use ammonia on glass decorated with gilt or enamel.)

Removing wax from candlesticks

- **Hot method** Re-melt wax with a hair dryer on the hot setting, and wipe the wax as it softens.
- **Cold method** Place candlesticks in the freezer for about an hour. This makes it easy to peel the wax off.

Burnt pans

- To clean a badly burnt saucepan, pour in a little olive oil, heat gently and leave to stand for 1 to 2 hours. Pour off the oil into a container, ready to use for the next burnt pan, and wash the pan as usual.
- To clean burnt food from a pie dish, dip it in very hot water then quickly turn it upside down onto a flat surface. This traps steam which loosens the residue.
- To restore a very burnt enamel baking dish, soak it in a mixture of water and strong soap powder. After a couple of hours, pour off the water and rub the dish with a soft cloth.

TEA AND SALT
To remove tea stains from china cups, rub crushed salt on with a dish cloth.

BONE CHINA AND PORCELAIN
Check the manufacturer's instructions as to the suitability of bone china and porcelain for the dishwasher. The harsh detergents used in dishwashers can spoil some glazes, especially metallic ones.

Greasy grill (broiler) pans

When you've scraped off as much grease as you can with a spatula or newspaper, sprinkle with washing soda crystals and pour on boiling water. Leave it to soak for at least 10 minutes, then clean up. The grease and debris just lift off.

Stained enamel

To whiten enamel-lined pans: finely crush egg shells and rub with a cloth dipped in salt if stained.

Delicate china

When hand-washing the heirloom china, place a towel at the bottom of the washing up bowl to help prevent chips and breakages.

Gilt china

Do not use washing soda or soap powder containing soda on gilt as it may damage it. Use a few drops of borax instead.

Cleaning coffee and teapots

- Wash all coffee-making equipment thoroughly after using.
- To de-scale a drip coffee maker, run a water and vinegar solution through the machine or use a shop-bought product.
- To remove stains, fill the pot with 1 part bicarbonate of soda to 2 parts hot water and leave to stand overnight. Rinse thoroughly and dry.
- A patina of tea inside the pot may add depth of flavour to the brew, but it can look ugly on the spout tip. Wrap a piece of nylon stocking around a pipe cleaner and dampen it with salty water. Use it to clean the spout.

- To remove tannin stains inside pottery teapots, fill with 1 cup salt to 2 cups water, soak overnight; rinse with hot water.

- To remove tannin stains from silver teapots, drop in 6 pieces of aluminium foil, add 1 tablespoon bicarbonate of soda and pour on boiling water. Leave to cool, then rinse out with hot water and dry with a soft cloth.

Premium care for pots and pans

Fill pots and pans with hot water as soon as they are emptied. For greasy pots, wash with a solution of washing soda and hot water. Saucepans that have contained rice, potato and porridge (oatmeal) are better soaked in cold water. Wipe out excess grease with newspaper.

- **Aluminium** To clean stained aluminium saucepans, boil up 2 teaspoons of cream of tartar with 4 cups of water. Apple peelings or citrus skin will also clean aluminium saucepans. Boil in the pan with water.

- **Bakeware** Baking trays and cake pans need to be seasoned like cast iron to prevent rusting. Do not scour. Check the manufacturer's instructions after purchase. After turning out biscuits (cookies) or cakes, fill bakeware with cold water, add a handful of washing soda and let it stand on a warm stove until the crust is loose and can be removed without scratching.

- **Cast iron** Season new pans by brushing the bottom of the pan with vegetable oil. Gently heat over a low flame or in the oven for an hour. Remove from the heat and allow to cool. Pour out the oil and discard, then wipe out the pan with paper towel. After using the pan, wash it in hot water and detergent, then dry. Brush on a little oil before storing.

- **Copper** Do not scour. Soak encrusted food in warm water. Clean off poisonous green stains. Clean the outside with a solution of 1 part salt and 2 parts white vinegar, rinse, then dry and polish.

- **Glazed earthenware** Soak in hot water and use a plastic scourer to remove food remains.

- **Unglazed earthenware** To season before first use, soak in water. Use hot water only, no detergent, to clean. Soak difficult stains but do not scour.

- **Enamel** Season as for cast iron. To clean, use a very gentle scouring pad. Bleach discoloured enamelware with a mixture of coarse salt and vinegar.

- **Glass** Heatproof glass baking ware and saucepans can go in the dishwasher. Use a plastic scourer when necessary.

- **Non-stick finishes** Soak to remove food; never use a scourer as it will scratch and remove the surface.

- **Plastic** Do not scratch by scouring as the scratches may harbour bacteria. Hand-hot water is fine, but dishwashers may get too hot.

- **Stainless steel** Scourers will scratch, but you may not be bothered by a patina of small scratches. Usually dishwasher safe. To remove calcium deposits, boil water and vinegar together.

Caring for knives

- **Blunt knives** Sharpening stones are best. Wash individually by hand in cold or lukewarm water, as hot water can warp blades. Dry thoroughly and store in a wooden knife block.

- **Rusty knives** Soak in raw linseed oil for a few hours then wipe off the rust. Polish the knife with emery paper.

- **Stained blades** Clean with emery paper rubbed with a slice of raw potato or salt and cut lemon. Alternatively, use a scouring pad.

- **Stained knife handles** Restore ivory handles by rubbing them with salt moistened with lemon juice.

Caring for metal

As a general rule, metal can be dusted and, if necessary, wiped with a cloth dampened in water or a mixture of water and an all-purpose cleanser such as detergent. Rinse and dry it at once, especially if it's a metal that is prone to rust.

- Iron, silver, copper and brass are prone to tarnish — that's when the surface of the metal reacts with a substance in the surrounding air, forming a discolouring compound. The process is accelerated by humidity and temperature.

- Gold, platinum, pewter, bronze, aluminium, stainless steel and chrome do not tarnish, although they can stain.

- Metal polishes may be all-purpose or specific for a particular metal. They contain abrasives or solvents; sometimes both. The more valuable a piece of metal, the more care you need to take when cleaning it, and the less eager you should be to use all-purpose 'all metals' cleaners. If you use solvents and abrasives that are too strong, you run the risk of losing detail on raised designs and etching as the top surface is likely to be removed.

Aluminium

- To brighten dull aluminium, boil 4 cups water with 4 tablespoons white vinegar.

- Harmful substances that will damage the metal include chlorine bleach, strong bicarbonate of soda solutions, and alkaline cleansers, including oven cleaners.

Brass

- Rub briskly with a cotton wool pad wrung out in vinegar, then wash thoroughly in hot soapy water. Rub dry with a soft towel.

- For mild tarnish, clean with a mixture of salt and lemon juice, then rinse. Use an old toothbrush to clean patterned areas.

TO LACQUER OR NOT TO LACQUER?
Bronze, brass and copper readily tarnish and need regular polishing unless lacquered. Once thoroughly cleaned and lacquered they will stay bright and tarnish-free. However, if cracks begin to appear in the lacquer it must be removed with acetone, the metal cleaned and lacquer reapplied. Paste wax and mineral oil both inhibit tarnishing, if you decide against lacquer.

- Try removing stubborn marks with Worcestershire sauce and salt; apply with a toothbrush, wash in warm water, dry well and rub with a clean cloth. If that doesn't work, try toothpaste on the toothbrush. Leave on for a while, rinse off with warm water and polish dry. Alternatively, try lemon juice and bicarbonate of soda or a paste of equal parts salt, white flour and vinegar. Rub on, leave for an hour and rinse off. Dry with a soft cloth then buff. Last, but not least, a simple piece without trimming and decoration can be boiled in a solution made from 1 tablespoon vinegar, 2 cups water and 1 tablespoon salt. Rinse and dry.

- To clean brass fireplace screens and tools, dust the soot off first, then wash in detergent and warm water. Rinse and dry with a soft cloth.

- A number of substances — including chlorine bleach, oven cleaners and some window cleaners — corrode and discolour brass.

Bronze

Do not wash bronze. Dust regularly with a soft cloth. Polish from time to time with a cloth dipped in boiled linseed oil. Buff with a soft dry cloth.

Cast iron

- Items not used for cooking can be protected with paste wax. Hinges and locks should be oiled with machine oil to prevent rust.

- Wash by hand and dry thoroughly after washing to prevent rusting: a few seconds on the stove top ensures all moisture evaporates.

- To remove rust, scour off and dry.

- To season cast iron pans, see page 116.

Copper

- Rub in a mixture of 2 tablespoons vinegar to 1 tablespoon salt. Plunge into hot water and rinse. Dry thoroughly with a soft cloth.

- Remove mild tarnish with salt and lemon juice, as for bronze, above.

- Never let copper stand in chlorine bleach for more than a few hours or the metal will become discoloured.

ACID DIPS AND ELECTROLYTIC CLEANERS

Acid dips can be rough on silver and are best used only for black tarnish that resists all other polishes. In addition, many experts advise wiping with the solution rather than immersing an object. Cracks and crevices filled with acid may continue to corrode, so wash a piece after using it.

Pieces cleaned by electrolytic cleansing are prone to tarnishing more quickly because they more readily absorb substances that tarnish. If you are tempted to use this method, ensure you wash the piece thoroughly afterwards to prevent solution being trapped in cracks.

Iron

- Wrought iron merely needs dusting, but it can be washed if necessary. Rub stubborn marks with steel wool. Paste wax gives extra shine and protection against rust. Apply to a thoroughly clean iron with a cloth, allow wax to dry, then buff with a clean cloth.

- To remove rust, wipe with a solution of white vinegar and water.

Pewter

- Wash in warm soapy water. To help keep pewter bright, add 2 tablespoons ammonia per 4 cups water.

- For stubborn marks, try mixing finely powdered artist's whiting (sold in art supply stores) with a little oil and apply with a soft cloth. Rub in well, then polish with a clean cloth and finally a chamois. Rinse in warm water. Wipe dry with a clean towel.

- Remove grease marks by rubbing with a cloth moistened with methylated spirits (denatured alcohol).

- Pewter is vulnerable to damage by acids, including those in oak and unseasoned wood, and in some food. If necessary, polish it with silver polish.

Silver

- Using silver is the best way to keep it looking bright; too much polishing can wear it out.

- Some foods tarnish silver, so wash silver or silver plate quickly after a meal. Items that contain sulphur tarnish silver. These include felt and chamois leather, as well as a number of foods.

- To wash silver, wash in very hot water and detergent. Rinse carefully (as soap residue can make it tarnish) and dry with a cloth rather than let it air dry, as water standing on silver causes tarnish.

- Rub egg stains on silver with wet salt.

- For other stains, use fine artist's whiting moistened with ammonia or alcohol then wash and polish.

- Clean tarnished silver plate with starch mixed with methylated spirits (denatured alcohol) to form a paste. Let it dry on the silver then rub off with a soft cloth.

- To remove wax on silver candlesticks, warm gently in the oven or with a hair dryer. Peel it off.

- To prevent silver tarnishing after cleaning, smear lightly with petroleum jelly — but remember, this must be washed off before the silver is used with food again.

- To clean the old-fashioned way, cover with sour milk for half an hour, wash and rinse.

- Remember to clean all silver thoroughly before polishing.

- To polish silver, use a commercial silver polish. Apply polish gently with a soft, clean cloth in a circular motion, polishing bit by bit for larger objects. Don't rub with a dirty cloth as the dirt can scratch — keep moving to a clean part of the cloth. Rinse polish off thoroughly with hot water as it can sometimes corrode silver, then buff with a soft cloth. (Don't leave to air dry.)

- Don't polish silver plate too vigorously or you may rub it off.

- For valuable antiques, commercial silver polish may be too harsh. Instead, use a paste of distilled water and artist's whiting.

- To store silver, you can buy cloths, bags and drawer liners that have been treated with silver nitrate or other chemicals to retard tarnish.

(It is not necessary to clean tarnish before storing; polishing up silver so that it is ready just before use will save time.)

- Plastic wrap can help retard tarnish too. The silver must be absolutely dry. It needs to be wrapped in archival quality, sulphur-free tissue paper before being packed in plastic. Place moisture-absorbing silica gel packets in the packaging and store out of direct sunlight.

Stainless steel

- Stainless steel may be damaged by salty or acidic substances such as vinegar and citrus juices as well as some dishwasher detergents and denture cleaners.

- Brown and blue streaks can occur with overheating; stainless steel cleaners will remove them.

- Small white dots or pits are produced by salted liquids. White dots will come off with a scouring pad or a soaped steel wool pad. Pits, however, are permanent. Prevent them by always bringing liquids to the boil before adding salt.

Refrigerating, freezing and storing food

The fridge and freezer are two of the most used items in the kitchen. But how many of us really know the rules for correct refrigeration and freezing? Here are some vital tips.

Using the fridge

The refrigeration of food inhibits the growth of spoiling micro-organisms and chemical changes in food. Most care is needed with foods of the flesh: meat, especially minced (ground) meat — liver, kidney, poultry and seafood. This is because these foods always contain large numbers of micro-organisms that can cause spoilage and food poisoning.

When buying chilled (or frozen) foods, wrap them in newspaper to keep temperature changes to a minimum while you're on your way home. Pack them in an insulated container if putting them away is likely to be delayed. Put chilled foods away immediately on returning home.

PUTTING HOT FOOD STRAIGHT INTO THE FRIDGE

Modern fridges can cope with large quantities of hot food without heating up other fridge contents. Cover the container, and if you are concerned the food will not cool quickly enough, you can always divide a large quantity into smaller amounts in shallow dishes.

DANGER ZONE

The range of temperatures that are conducive to bacterial growth is broad — between 4°C and 60°C (39.2°F and 140°F). Bacteria are an omnipresent fact of life. They are present in most foods at harmless levels, and on your hands, arms, face and inside your body too. In addition, many bacteria are harmless. But high levels of harmful bacteria can make you ill and may even kill you. The danger comes when harmful bacteria are transferred to foods where they can multiply quickly and reach a hazardously high concentration. Transfer of bacteria from uncooked foods to cooked foods is particularly dangerous, as the cooked foods may not be heated again to destroy bacteria.

The most important principles of food hygiene are aimed at minimizing the time food spends in the danger zone.

- Keep food hot — above 60°C (140°F) — if it's to be served hot.

- Refrigerate food after cooking if it is not going to be eaten immediately.

- When reheating, ensure the centre of the food reaches 75°C (167°F) to kill any bacteria present.

Temperature	Comment
100°C (212°F)	Boiling point cooking temperatures destroy most bacteria
60–74°C (140–165.2°F)	Warming temperatures prevent growth but allow survival of some bacteria
4–60°C (39.2–140°F)	Danger zone: temperatures in this zone allow rapid growth of bacteria, including food-poisoning bacteria
0–4°C (32–39.2°F)	Chilling temperatures restrict growth. Some food-poisoning bacteria may grow very slowly
0°C (32°F)	Freezing point
–12°C (10.4°F)	Freezing temperatures stop the growth of bacteria

FRIDGE HYGIENE

■ Store food you want to keep for a long time and foods such as seafood in the coldest part of the fridge.

■ Store cooked foods above uncooked ones: this minimizes the risk of food poisoning by drips from the uncooked foods.

■ Wrap foods with strong odours, such as seafood and cheese, and avoid storing them close to milk and cream, which are susceptible to tainting.

■ Throw out food going off: the slimy lettuce at the back of the fridge can taint other food.

Recommended storage times and temperatures for refrigerated foods

FOOD	TEMPERATURE	KEEP FOR
Seafood	0–3°C (32–37.4°F)	3 days
Crustaceans and molluscs	0–3°C (32–37.4°F)	2 days
Meat	0–3°C (32–37.4°F)	3–5 days
Minced (ground) meat and offal (variety meats)	0–3°C (32–37.4°F)	2–3 days
Cured meat	0–3°C (32–37.4°F)	2–3 weeks
Poultry	0–3°C (32–37.4°F)	3 days
Fruit juices	0–7°C (32–44.6°F)	1–2 weeks
Milk	1–7°C (33.8–44.6°F)	5–7 days
Cream	1–7°C (33.8–44.6°F)	5–7 days
Butter	0–7°C (32–44.6°F)	8 weeks
Oil and fat	2–7°C (35.6–44.6°F)	approx. 6 months
Chilled meats and meals	0–3°C (32–37.4°F)	up to use-by date
Leftovers	0–3°C (32–37.4°F)	3–5 days

Source: CSIRO and AFSIC, 'Handling food: The home', *Food Science Australia*, March 2000.

FAST THAW
If you don't have time to thaw meat in the fridge, the next-safest method is under cool, running water or in the microwave oven. If you are not sure that all portions of the meat have thawed, use a meat thermometer when cooking to check that the interior reaches 75°C (167°F).

Freezing rules

Freezers run at around –18°C (0.4°F), a temperature which almost, but not quite, prevents foods from deteriorating.

- **Freeze fast** Put frozen foods away as soon as you get home from the shops.

- **To thaw or not to thaw?** Vegetables can be cooked from the frozen state. Many have been blanched before freezing and need only light cooking. Always completely thaw meat and poultry to avoid the possibility of starting cooking with a frozen patch which then does not reach a bacteria-killing temperature.

- **Thaw in the fridge** Food hygiene experts say never to thaw meat out of the fridge because it may reach 4°C (39.2°F) — the temperature at which bacteria starts to breed, potentially causing spoilage and food poisoning. This means allowing 24 to 48 hours for a large piece of meat, or a whole chicken, to thaw in the fridge.

- **Cook immediately** If you thaw meat out of the fridge, don't be tempted to put it in the fridge once you have thawed it: you must cook it immediately to avoid food poisoning.

- **Don't refreeze** Once thawed correctly (in the fridge), food can be kept another 48 hours in the fridge, but it should never be refrozen.

HOARDING IN THE FREEZER
While a well-stocked freezer may be highly convenient, long-term hoarding of packaged frozen goods is not a good idea. It's better to stock less and buy more often, as a shop's freezing cabinets hold food at a lower temperature than home freezers can offer.

Freezing chart

1–2 MONTHS

Bread (sliced)	Shellfish (raw and cooked)
Milk	Scones (biscuits) (unbaked)
Soups	Cakes (unbaked)
Stews	Biscuits (cookies) (unbaked)
Sausages	Sandwiches (2 weeks to a month,
Pancakes, pikelets and waffles	depending on the filling)

2–3 MONTHS

Cream	Offal (variety meats) and bacon
Cottage cheese	Oily fish (sardines, trout, mullet)
Cakes	Filled pies (unbaked)
Scones (biscuits)	Minced (ground) meats (except beef)
Ice cream	Poultry giblets
Bread (unbaked)	Leftover dishes
Pastry (baked and unbaked)	

3–4 MONTHS

Ham	Butter (salted)
Lamb	White-fleshed fish
Cheddar cheese, grated	Fruit cake (unbaked)

4–6 MONTHS

Minced (ground) beef	Butter (unsalted)
Veal	Pork
Game	

6–8 MONTHS

Bread (unsliced)	Pizza
Biscuits (cookies)	Filled pies

8–12 MONTHS

Beef	Fruit cake
Poultry	Vegetables
Fruit	

Storing dried goods

Dehydration slows down deterioration of food, but once the foods are exposed to water again — even when packets are open to the air — the microbes present in the food become active again. Dried food keeps in an unopened container for about 6 months when stored at 21–24°C (69.8–75.2°F).

- Store dried goods in a cool place away from sources of heat or direct sunlight. Inspect regularly for contamination.
- Opened packages of dried fruit will keep for longer in the fridge.
- Once dehydrated foods, such as dips, are reconstituted, treat them as fresh food and refrigerate them.

How long can you keep cans?

Most canned food can be safely kept for 12 months, if not longer, when stored at 21–24°C (69.8–75.2°F). Exceptions are rhubarb, fruit juices, soft drinks and some baby foods, which have a maximum storage life of 6 months. Keep an eye on the use-by dates and remember to rotate pantry items so that you use the oldest first.

Which cooking methods are more likely to trigger allergy problems?

- Electricity produces fewer combustion by-products and less water vapour than cooking with gas or solid fuel, and is generally considered the better choice for allergy sufferers.
- Burning gas produces water vapour and chemicals such as carbon monoxide, carbon dioxide, nitrogen dioxide, sulphur dioxide and aldehydes. Ensure the kitchen is well ventilated for all the family.
- Ducted hoods are vented to the outside, removing combustion by-products and excess condensation. An open window or a window ventilator prevents air being sucked from the rest of the house. Recirculating hoods send air back into the kitchen after passing it through a filter. They remove grease and odours but not moisture.

THE CLEVER SHOPPING BASKET

When shopping for food, always avoid the following:

■ **Swollen chilled food packages** This occurs in fruit juices, yoghurts and unprocessed cheese, and is a sign that the food is going off, being overpopulated with micro-organisms which are producing gas.

■ **Swollen and severely dented cans** Swollen cans can indicate the same problem as swollen chilled food packages — a fault in the original processing has allowed bacteria to multiply. Badly damaged cans could indicate that the can is no longer properly sealed.

■ **Dairy produce or delicatessen items not kept under refrigeration** These items should always be cold on purchase.

■ **Refrigerated foods past their use-by date** This group of items presents a risk of food poisoning.

■ **Frozen and refrigerated foods stored outside the load line of the display cabinet** Foods will keep to the correct storage temperature only below the 'load' line, usually about 5 cm (2 inches) below the rim of the cabinet.

■ **Frozen food packs with ice crystals or clumps of ice between them** This indicates refreezing, which usually means loss of quality.

■ **Torn packaging or imperfect seals** There is probably a deterioration of quality of the food.

What to keep in the store cupboard

Although it is best to shop regularly for meat, seafood and seasonal vegetables, there are certain products that you will want to keep permanently in your store cupboard, to provide the backbone of your daily cooking. As a general rule, you should try to have in your pantry:

- Baking powder
- Beans, canned and dried
- Breadcrumbs, dry
- Capers
- Cocoa powder
- Coconut milk (cream)
- Cornflour (cornstarch)
- Oils (olive, sesame, vegetable)
- Olives (in a jar)
- Pasta
- Polenta
- Rice, long-grain, short-grain and arborio (risotto)
- Soy sauce

- Couscous
- Dried fruits, such as raisins, currants, apricots
- Flour (plain and self-raising)
- Gelatine
- Honey
- Mustards
- Noodles
- Nuts
- Stocks
- Sugars
- Tabasco
- Tomatoes, canned
- Tomato paste
- Vinegars, white wine, red wine, brown and balsamic
- Worcestershire sauce
- Yeast

Food fundamentals

Knowing what to look for when buying fresh ingredients is essential, as is correct handling. Following are some specific tips on buying, storing and preparation of meat, fish and vegetables.

Buying and storing meat

Correct handling and preparation of meat is crucial, both for safety reasons and for good eating. When buying, look for meat that has a clear, fresh appearance: meat with a greyish tinge has been poorly handled and stored and must be avoided. An unpleasant odour and slimy surface are other indicators that the product is unacceptable. Offal (variety meats) such as kidneys and liver that have a strong smell of ammonia should be rejected.

Meat should be kept refrigerated, so buy it last on your shopping trip and bring it straight home. Unwrap the meat and put it on a plate, then loosely wrap it with foil or greaseproof paper and place it in the refrigerator. Be sure to use within a couple of days.

Meats wrapped in plastic do not last as well as unwrapped meat because they contain more water and the wrapping encourages bacterial growth at the surface, which can become slimy after about 3 days. Throw it out if this happens.

The surface of unwrapped meat dries out, which actually discourages bacterial growth — although it is less attractive looking and may lose some flavour. To keep meat covered without letting anything come into

Food storage chart

INGREDIENTS	IN THE FRIDGE	SPECIAL REQUIREMENTS
Butter	Wrap tightly to stop it becoming tainted or going rancid.	Unsalted butter will not last as long as salted butter.
Dairy, such as milk and cream	Keep cartons and bottles closed as milk taints very easily.	
Eggs	Keep in the box in which they are sold as they easily taint from other smells in the fridge.	Do not store loose in the egg holes.
Fish	Put on a plate, cover with plastic wrap and keep for as short a time as possible.	Gut fish before storage as ungutted fish go off quickly.
Fruit	Store in the salad compartment. Strong-smelling fruit like melon should be tightly wrapped if it is cut or it will taint other things.	Bananas and avocados should be stored in cool places but not the fridge, if possible.
Herbs	Store in their plastic bags or containers in the salad compartment or put large bunches in a jug of water.	Buy pot herbs if you can, as you often only need a few leaves out of each bunch. This way, you can pick them as you need them.
Meat	Remove from packaging, put on a plate and cover with plastic wrap.	Store on the bottom shelf of the fridge so no blood can drip onto cooked food.
Poultry	If there are giblets included, remove them as soon as you get home. Unwrap the chicken, put it on a plate and cover with plastic wrap.	Store on the bottom shelf of the fridge so no blood can drip onto cooked food.
Shellfish	Store in the salad compartment in a bowl and cover with a damp cloth.	Do not put in cold water if alive or they will drown.
Vegetables	Store in the salad compartment.	Root vegetables should be stored in the dark.

contact with the surface, place it in a ceramic bowl covered with greaseproof paper, plastic wrap or a plate.

Meat also freezes very successfully if you need to store it for longer. Remove the original wrapping and seal the meat in a freezer bag, first expelling as much air as possible. Double-bag the meat if there is any danger of the bag tearing, as meat exposed to air will suffer from freezer burn. Clearly label the bag, including the date. Most cuts of meat can be frozen for up to 6 months.

There is a huge variety of meat available. The main types are beef, veal, lamb and pork. Within these types there are myriad cuts, and each cut has its most suitable cooking method. Buy the appropriate cut for the cooking process you will be using. Each cut has distinctive qualities that can be used to advantage in a specific instance. Don't buy a cut that is more expensive than you need — a cheaper one may well give a better result in your particular recipe.

Different types of meat and cooking methods require different preparation. A general first step in meat preparation is to remove the meat from the refrigerator a little while before cooking, to allow it to cool to room temperature. This ensures the meat will cook evenly and quickly, which is particularly important when using a quick cooking method such as pan-frying a steak. Sometimes the recipe will instruct you to cut away any visible fat and sinew, particularly when stewing. However, sometimes some fat present on the meat can be desirable, for instance when you are cooking a roast — the fat will melt and baste the meat as it cooks, contributing to the tenderness and flavour.

Take extra care with cooked meat

One of the most common sources of food poisoning is cold cooked meat, often by cross-contamination from knives, hands and chopping boards.

- Never handle cooked and uncooked meats together.
- When preparing cooked and uncooked meats, either use different chopping boards and utensils, or thoroughly wash and dry them before switching foods.

How much do I need to buy?

This chart will help you to gauge how much of something to buy per head. The quantities are quite generous, but the more dishes you serve at once, the less you will need per person. The meat and fish quantities are for a single main course.

INGREDIENTS	QUANTITIES
Batter, pancake or crêpe	110 g (3¾ oz) (flour quantity) makes about 12 crêpes
Beef, fillet (tenderloin)	200 g (7 oz) per person
Beef, joint off the bone	200 g (7 oz) per person
Beef, joint on the bone	320 g (11¼ oz) per person
Beef, steaks	200 g (7 oz) each. Steaks with bones weigh more
Beef and veal, cubed or sliced	200–225 g (7–8 oz) each (trimmed weight)
Canapés	4 to 5 canapés per head with drinks, 10 to 14 canapés per head if no other food is served
Chicken, breasts	1 breast each, but if sliced, 3 x 175 g (6 oz) breasts will feed 4 people
Chicken, whole	1 large (1.5 kg/3 lb 5 oz) chicken per 4 people for roasting/chicken per person for casseroles
Fish, fillets	175–200 g (6–7 oz) each
Fish, whole (individual, such as trout)	250–300 g (9–10½ oz) each
Fish, whole (large, such as salmon)	350–400 g (12–14 oz) per person
Lamb, chops	2 per person
Lamb, cubed or sliced	225 g (8 oz) each (trimmed weight)
Lamb, cutlets	3 to 4 each
Lamb, leg or shoulder on the bone	400–500 g (14 oz to 1 lb 2 oz) per person

INGREDIENTS	QUANTITIES
Mince (ground) meat, all types	175 g (6 oz) per person for hamburgers, pies etc., 110 g (3¾ oz) per person for chilli con carne and spaghetti Bolognese
Pasta	70 g (2½ oz) per head for a small portion, 100 g (3½ oz) for a normal portion, 150 g (5½ oz) for a large portion
Pastry, puff and flaky	500 g (1 lb 2 oz) pastry (made with 225 g/8 oz flour) makes 1 millefeuille, 4 tarts or covers 1 pie
Pastry, shortcrust and sweet	225 g (8 oz) pastry (made with 175 g/6 oz flour) lines a 20 cm (8 in) tart pan, 325 g (11½ oz) pastry (made with 225 g/8 oz flour) lines a 25 cm/10 in tart pan
Pork, chops	1 x 175–225 g (6–8 oz) chop per person
Pork, cubed or sliced	200–225 g (7–8 oz) per person
Pork, joint off the bone	200 g (7 oz) per person
Pork, joint on the bone	320 g (11¼ oz) per person
Potato	110–185 g (3¾–6½ oz) per head
Prawns (shrimp), shell on	150 g (5½ oz) per head as a starter and 300 g (10½ oz) as a main
Prawns (shrimp), shelled	85 g (3 oz) per head as a starter and 150 g (5½ oz) as a main
Rice	55 g (2 oz) uncooked per head for boiled or fried rice. 30 g (1 oz) uncooked per head for risotto
Soup	300 ml (10½ fl oz) per head as a starter and 500 ml (17 fl oz/2 cups) as a main course

Buying and storing chicken

Free-range and corn-fed chickens are now widely available and have a better flavour and texture than intensively farmed chickens. Free-range chickens can be identified by a label stating that they have been reared humanely. Corn-fed chickens have a yellowy skin and flesh, but are not necessarily free-range. You will, of course, pay more for a free-range bird, but it will have a better flavour.

Whole chickens are sold by a number that relates to their weight, for example, a no.15 chicken will weigh 1.5 kg (3 lb) and should feed 4 people. Larger birds will feed 4 to 6.

Breasts can be bought on the bone or as 'fillets' (bone removed) — both are available as single or double, joined breasts, sometimes with the skin on. Breasts will have a small tenderloin underneath.

Thighs have darker, more succulent meat than breasts, work well in curries and stews and for kebabs and satays. Thigh cutlets have both skin and a thigh bone, thigh fillets have no skin or bone, and thighs have some backbone and an 'oyster'.

Make chicken one of the last items to be bought and have it out of the fridge for the shortest possible time. Frozen chicken must be solid and tightly wrapped. Fresh chicken should be taken out of its packaging, covered loosely with plastic wrap and put on a plate to catch any drips. Keep it in the fridge, and not where it can drip onto other food. Cook it within 2 days.

Chicken can be frozen for up to 3 months, sealed in a freezer bag with the air expelled (make sure you write the date on a label). Thaw chicken carefully as bacteria, such as salmonella, can be activated if it gets too warm. Thaw in the fridge, not at room temperature. Chicken pieces can be thawed in the microwave (arrange the thickest portions to the outside of the plate). Don't thaw whole birds in the microwave — they thaw unevenly and some parts may start to cook. Use thawed chicken within 12 hours and never refreeze. Cooked chicken can be kept in the fridge for up to 3 days.

Buying and storing fish and seafood

Fish and seafood are highly perishable and care must be taken when shopping for, storing and preparing these food items.

Ideally seafood should be the last thing you buy on your shopping trip, to ensure the shortest time possible out of refrigeration. Your fishseller should wrap the seafood in a plastic bag to keep in the moisture and then several insulating layers of paper. While you pretty much have to take your fishseller's word for the freshness of his wares, there are some general signs to look for. Fresh fish should have bulging and clear eyes, not sunken and cloudy. The skin should be plump and moist. Fish fillets should be plump, moist and evenly coloured. There should be no dry edges. Shellfish such as lobsters and crabs are generally best bought live, though they are also available already cooked or frozen. If you are buying them live, they should be fairly active. If you are buying them cooked, make sure the shell is intact and there is no discolouration around the joints. Fresh, raw prawns (shrimp) should be plump and firm (not mushy), and without black spots. Cooked prawns should have a firm head and shell, and no black discolouration. Generally, all seafood should have a pleasant, characteristically fresh, fishy smell. Avoid anything that looks or smells at all unappealing.

Seafood has a very short storage life and is best used within a day of purchase. Place fish on a plate, to prevent dripping onto other foods, cover with plastic wrap or foil and store in the fridge. Seafood can actually given an undesirable smell to other foods — another reason not to store it for too long. Seafood can be frozen, if absolutely necessary. It is a great way to store fish you have caught yourself, as you can be assured of the freshness. If freezing bought fish, check with the fishseller whether it has already been frozen and thawed — if it has been, don't ever refreeze it (this applies to all food to be frozen, not just seafood).

- **Fish** Fish can be frozen whole, but must be cleaned first, and rinsed to remove any traces of blood (pat dry with paper towels). If a white fish is going to be filleted, then do so before freezing. Put the fish into a freezer bag and extract as much air as possible. Seal firmly and clearly label with the date. To make separation easier when you come to use frozen fillets, place a sheet of freezer wrap between them. Freeze non-oily fish for up to 4 months and oily fish for up to 3 months.

- **Shellfish** Lobsters, crabs, prawns (shrimp) and other crayfish can be frozen raw or cooked, and don't need to be cleaned first. Wrap larger shellfish in plastic wrap or foil, then in a freezer bag, extracting as much air as possible. Take care that any sharp parts of the shell don't pierce the bag. Freeze for up to 2 months.

- **Squid and octopus** Clean and cut into pieces for cooking. Freeze raw, in a freezer bag with as much air extracted as possible. Freeze for up to 4 months.

- **Molluscs** Mussels, oysters, scallops, pipis and clams should be cooked and the meat frozen, without the shell, in a freezer bag with as much air extracted as possible. Freeze for up to 3 months.

Thawing fish and seafood

There is no need to thaw small or thin fillets of fish, just cook a little longer than the given time. If the fillet is to have further preparation, such as coating with crumbs or batter, just thaw enough to make it easy to handle. Alternatively, fish can be crumbed before freezing — the coating sticks better this way and there is no need to thaw. Other seafood should be thawed in the fridge, never at room temperature, and never in a sink full of water. Cook any seafood as soon as it has thawed.

Preparing vegetables

- **Asparagus** To remove the sometimes tough and woody end of the asparagus, bend the stem end of each spear. It will snap where it begins to get tough. Blanch to use in salads or, if very tender, use raw. Blanching makes vegetables such as asparagus and snow peas (mangetout) tender without cooking them, and preserves the bright colour. To do this, place the vegetables in a pan and cover with boiling water (it's easier to tie asparagus together into a bunch). Leave for 30–60 seconds, depending on the size. Drain, then plunge into iced water. Drain again and pat dry.

- **Beans** Trim both ends of the bean ('top and tail') and remove the fibrous string that runs down each side, if necessary. Steam, boil or microwave until tender.

- **Beetroot (beet)** Raw beetroot will stain, so take care. Trim the stalks to 2 cm (¾ inch) above the bulb, leaving the skin intact. Boil whole until tender, then cool and slip off the skins. Also good raw, peeled and grated.

- **Broccoli** Cut into florets (make them fairly small if stir-frying) and steam, boil or microwave until tender.

- **Brussels sprouts** Remove any tough or yellow outer leaves and score a cross in the base so the sprout cooks all the way through. Steam, boil or microwave until tender.

- **Cabbage** Remove any tough outer leaves and chop or shred the inner leaves. Serve raw and shredded in coleslaw, or steam, microwave or stir-fry very briefly.

- **Capsicum (pepper)** Cut into quarters and remove the seeds and white membrane. Serve raw or stir-fry, or leave whole and stuff. Removing the skin from capsicums by grilling (broiling) or roasting makes the flavour of the flesh even sweeter. Cut the capsicums into large, flattish pieces, removing the seeds and membrane. Place, skin-side up, under a hot grill (broiler) until the skin is black and blistered. Put in a plastic bag or under a tea towel to cool — this steams and loosens the skin, which can be peeled away.

- **Carrots** Scrub the skin or peel if you like. Serve raw or steam, boil, microwave, roast or stir-fry.

- **Cauliflower** Cut into florets. Steam, boil, microwave or stir-fry.

- **Celery** Trim the stalks, removing the leaves and thick root end. Good raw, stir-fried or in soups or stews.

- **Corn** Remove the outer husk and silk. Boil or microwave, but don't overcook or the corn will become tough. Also good roasted, either in foil, or in the husk: peel back the husk and remove the silk, then pull the husk back into place to cover the kernels and roast.

- **Eggplant (aubergine)** The flesh from large eggplants can contain bitter juices — this is why many recipes will tell you to chop the flesh, put in a colander and sprinkle generously with salt to draw out the juice. Leave for 20 minutes, then rinse and pat dry. Fry, stir-fry or cook in curries or stews.

- **Mushrooms** Don't wash mushrooms before cooking or they will become soggy. Wipe clean with paper towel or peel, if necessary.

- **Parsnip** Peel and cut off the stalk end. Steam, microwave, roast or boil, as for potatoes.

- **Peas** Remove from the pod and boil or steam until tender.

- **Potatoes** Peel or scrub the skin, removing any 'eyes'. Use either a floury or waxy variety if stated in the recipe.

- **Pumpkin** Peel and remove the seeds and membrane, then steam, boil or microwave. If you are roasting pumpkin, you don't need to peel it first — the peel is easier to remove after.

- **Snow peas (mangetout)** Top and tail, then stir-fry or serve them raw or blanched.

- **Sweet potato** Peel and then steam, microwave, boil or roast. Mash just like potatoes. Also good roasted in the skin, after which the soft flesh can be scooped out.

- **Tomato** Serve raw in salads, or fry, grill (broil), or roast. Recipes will occasionally ask for tomatoes to be peeled, particularly in sauces where the peel can add an unpleasant texture. To do this, score a cross in the base of each tomato. Put in a heatproof bowl and cover with boiling water. Leave for about 1 minute (the ripeness of the tomato will determine how easily the skin comes away), then transfer to a bowl of cold water. Peel the skin away from the cross. To remove the seeds, cut in half horizontally and scoop them out with a teaspoon.

- **Zucchini (courgette)** Trim the ends and chop. Steam, stir-fry or cook in curries or stews.

A cook's tools

A good cook needs good tools. Buy the best you can afford and look after them and they'll last you for years.

- **Knives** Quality knives are expensive but it is well worth saving up for stainless steel or carbon steel knives. To keep your knives sharp, you should use a steel and stone and make sure you cut on a chopping board.

- **Whisk** A wire whisk is essential for beating egg whites — nothing else can incorporate as much air.

- **Large metal spoon** Ideal for folding mixtures together without losing volume, and skimming froth from stocks.

- **Wooden spoon** Perfect for long stirring jobs, since their handles don't get hot. Best for use with non-stick pans.

- **Spatula** Flexible rubber spatulas are ideal for folding in, and for getting every bit of cake mix out of the bowl.

- **Tongs** Use tongs to turn frying food or pick vegetables out of boiling water.

- **Peeler** Peels vegetable skins and the tip removes 'eyes' from potatoes. Also shaves Parmesan.

- **Ladle** For safely spooning hot soups and stews from a pan.

- **Rolling pin** Rolls pastry and pizza dough; beats veal, chicken or steak to flatten fillets; and crushes biscuits (cookies).

- **Saucepans** Stainless steel is the best material, even better if it has a heavy copper base. Most recipes state a 'heavy-based pan' as this distributes heat more evenly. A very large saucepan or stock pot is needed to cook pasta and stock.

- **Frying pan** A non-stick, deep frying pan will reduce the amount of oil needed and can be used for stir-frying if you don't have a wok. An ovenproof pan with a metal handle can go straight from stove top to oven or grill (broiler) for browning. Otherwise, cover the handle with foil.

- **Baking dish** You'll need a baking dish for roasting meat and vegetables. Buy one with a rack so the fat can drip down into the pan. Make sure it's heavy enough to put on top of the stove without warping. When stirring gravy, use a plastic or a wooden spoon to prevent scratching.

- **Mixing bowls** The best all-purpose mixing bowls also double as pudding basins. Use them to make cakes, beat cream, and a hundred other kitchen tasks. As long as they have no metal trim, china or ceramic mixing bowls are ideal for cooking or heating food in a microwave.

- **Casserole dish** Make sure your casserole dish has a tight-fitting lid and is a generous size. You can use ceramic dishes for oven only, but a good flameproof dish, as shown, can go straight from oven to stove top if you need to reduce a sauce over heat. Pyrex casserole dishes are also available.

- **Colander** Ideal for draining pasta, vegtables or anything else cooked in liquid (except small items, such as rice, which may need a strainer). Also ideal for washing salad leaves or placing on top of a saucepan to steam vegetables.

Microwaving

Microwave ovens have been in our kitchens for many years now, but for most of us they are still simply a means to thaw chicken in an emergency or warm up a forgotten cup of coffee. The microwave oven should be far more than that — it is a quick and fuss-free way to cook real family meals.

Microwave-safe dishes

There's no need to rush out and buy special cooking dishes for your microwave. The kitchen cupboard is probably full of bowls and casserole

DON'T USE THE MICROWAVE WHEN IT'S EMPTY
Do not turn on your microwave when it's empty, or you will damage the magnetron. If you have small children who may turn it on by accident, always leave a jug of water in the oven.

ARCING

Arcing occurs when metal blocks the passage of the microwaves and causes sparks to appear in the oven. This also happens if metal or aluminium foil touches the top, bottom or sides of the oven while it is operating. Repeated arcing can damage the oven.

dishes which are ideal. All ovenproof glass containers are suitable. Do not put anything metal into the microwave — this includes dishes with gold or silver trims and enamelled pots which have metal cores — but most other materials will be suitable. Even paper or plastic plates, wooden or wicker baskets can be used for just warming up food. You can test if a dish is suitable for cooking in the microwave by placing a jug of water in the microwave and putting the empty dish beside it (but not touching). Heat on High (100%) for 1 minute. If the water in the jug is hot and the empty dish cold then it is suitable for microwave cooking. If the empty dish is hot it has a high moisture content and is not suitable for microwaving. If it is warm, use the dish for reheating only.

Round containers are best for microwaving as they receive an even amount of microwave energy. Square containers tend to accumulate heat in the corners and overcook there.

You will notice in some recipes that you are instructed to use a dish which is both microwave-safe and ovenproof or heatproof — this is because the food may be browned under a grill (broiler) after microwaving, to give a crisp finish.

A word of warning: even though the dish itself should not heat up in the microwave oven, it will do so through contact with the food it contains. Always use oven gloves when removing dishes from the microwave.

Piercing

Any foods with a skin or membrane need to be pierced before being cooked whole in the microwave. The classic example of this is the baked potato, whose skin must be pricked before cooking to avoid pressure building up and causing it to burst (in exactly the same way that we pierce sausage skins before cooking to prevent them bursting open). Unshelled eggs should never be heated in the microwave.

Arranging the food

On a regular hot plate on the stove top the centre of the pan is the hottest, but in a microwave oven the food around the outside of the dish cooks the quickest. Always cut food into even-sized pieces and place it in a circle so that it cooks at the same rate. Put the thickest, and therefore slowest cooking, part of the food towards the outside of the dish — so chicken drumsticks, broccoli florets or whole fish would all be arranged with their thinnest parts pointing towards the centre of the dish. When cooking two ingredients of different sizes, for example cauliflower florets and peas, arrange the larger food around the edge of the dish and the smaller in the centre.

Stirring

Simple as it may seem, stirring is one of the most important techniques in microwave cooking. Because food around the outside of the dish cooks fastest, it needs to be stirred or rearranged to ensure even cooking. With stews and casseroles, always follow the instructions for stirring as it also helps the dish to thicken.

Covering

The golden rule is that any dish which you would normally cover in the conventional oven or on the stove top should be covered (either with a lid or with microwave-safe plastic wrap) in the microwave. Some people are tempted to cover everything they put in the microwave, but this just means that they are steaming rather than cooking, so follow the instructions in the recipe. Just as on the stove top, some dishes should be cooked uncovered to allow liquid to reduce and thicken.

You will find in a few recipes you are required to cover a dish tightly. This means with a close-fitting lid or a layer of microwave-safe plastic wrap. If instructed to 'cover' or 'cover loosely' you should use plastic wrap and leave one corner unsealed or make a couple of holes in the top with a sharp knife. When a dish does produce a lot of steam, make sure you remove the wrap away from you to avoid steam burns to your face.

Contrary to popular belief, aluminium foil can be used to cover small areas of food in the microwave oven. The foil must cover less than 30 per cent of the food (it is useful for very thin bits such as chicken wings or the tail of a fish, which may otherwise overcook), but it must never touch the side of the microwave oven.

Sometimes food is covered with paper towel while cooking. This is often food which may spit or release a lot of fat as it cooks. Check that your paper towel is microwave-safe: some recycled varieties are not.

After cooking

In many recipes you will be instructed to leave the dish to stand for several minutes before serving. This is an important part of microwave cooking — the heat that remains within the food causes it to continue cooking. Always follow these instructions in the recipe, as the standing time has been taken into account when calculating cooking times.

Browning

One of the main problems associated with cooking in the microwave is that the food doesn't brown and get the same lovely crunchy finish as you would if cooking in a regular oven. There are several ways to get round this. Sometimes meat or vegetables are basted or coated with seasoning before cooking to give a brown finish. Microwave browning pans are also available but it is just as simple to use a frying pan. Combine the speed and efficiency of microwave cooking with the crunchy smoky results from the frying pan or grill (broiler) by browning meat or vegetables in oil in a pan first or flashing a cheesy or breadcrumb topping under a hot grill after cooking.

Cleaning

Forget all the other advantages of the microwave over the conventional oven — all you really need to know is that it is a joy to clean. Simply put a large microwave-safe bowl or jug full of water into the oven, add a touch of lemon juice and a drop of ordinary dishwashing detergent and boil on High (100%) for 20 minutes. Do not cover or the water will boil over — also you want to produce lots of moisture. Remove the jug and wipe over the oven with a damp cloth — the dirt and grease will all have been loosened. Never use a commercial oven cleaner to clean the microwave oven.

Quick and easy vegetables from the microwave

A microwave oven really comes into its own when used to cook vegetables. Put the vegetable in a microwave-safe dish with the quantity of water or butter given. Cover with a lid or microwave-safe plastic wrap and cook on High (100%) for the stated time. Because of the speed of cooking, the vegetables retain their colour and nutrients.

ASPARAGUS

Quantity: 250 g (9 oz)

Preparation: Trim any woody ends from the spears. Add 3 tablespoons water.

Cooking time: 2–3 minutes

Serves 4

BEANS

Quantity: 250 g (9 oz)

Preparation: Top and tail. Add 1–2 tablespoons water.

Cooking time: 3–4 minutes

Serves 4

BROCCOLI

Quantity: 250 g (9 oz)

Preparation: Cut into florets and make a cut in the base of each stalk. Add 2 tablespoons water.

Cooking time: 3–4 minutes

Serves 4–6

BRUSSELS SPROUTS

Quantity: 250 g (9 oz)

Preparation: Remove any tough outer leaves and score a cross in the base of each sprout. Add 2 tablespoons water.

Cooking time: 3–4 minutes

Serves 4–6

CABBAGE

Quantity: Half a cabbage

Preparation: Cut into shreds. Use only the water clinging to the cabbage after washing, add a small knob of butter if you like.

Cooking time: 6–8 minutes

Serves 6

CARROTS

Quantity: 250 g (9 oz)

Preparation: Peel or scrub and cut into slices. Add 2 tablespoons water.

Cooking time: 3–4 minutes

Serves 4

CAULIFLOWER

Quantity: Half a cauliflower

Preparation: Cut into florets, and make a cut in the base of each stalk. Add 2 tablespoons water.

Cooking time: 7–8 minutes

Serves 4–6

CORN

Quantity: 2 cobs

Preparation: Remove husks and silk, dot with butter and wrap in microwave-safe plastic wrap.

Cooking time: 6–8 minutes

Serves 2

MUSHROOMS

Quantity: 250 g (9 oz)

Preparation: Wipe clean with paper towel and leave whole or slice if preferred. Dot with butter.

Cooking time: 3–5 minutes

Serves 4

ONIONS

Quantity: 250 g (9 oz)

Preparation: Slice finely. Add 1 tablespoon butter.

Cooking time: 3–4 minutes

Serves 4–6

PARSNIP

Quantity: 250 g (9 oz)

Preparation: Peel and slice. Add 2 tablespoons water.

Cooking time: 5–6 minutes

Serves 4

POTATOES

Quantity: 250 g (9 oz)

Preparation: Peel or scrub and cut into quarters. Add 2 tablespoons water.

Cooking time: 6–8 minutes

Serves 2

PUMPKIN

Quantity: 250 g (9 oz)

Preparation: Remove skin and seeds; cut into serving pieces. Add 2 tablespoons water.

Cooking time: 4–6 minutes

Serves 4

ZUCCHINI (COURGETTE)

Quantity: 250 g (9 oz)

Preparation: Trim ends and cut into thick slices. Dot with butter.

Cooking time: 3–4 minutes

Serves 4

Adapting recipes

One thing to beware of with microwave recipes is that you can't just double the quantities to make double the amount, as with conventional cooking. Liquid slows cooking times and fats and sugars cook at different rates, so the equation is not straightforward. Also, it is useful to remember that, although in a conventional oven two fish would take the same time to cook as one, in the microwave they will take proportionately longer — as they are both now sharing the same amount of microwaves, so each fish is receiving less.

Storing wine

Storage conditions are important if wine is to be kept for any length of time as the conditions affect how the wine ages. Put your wine rack in the best possible place in your home and you'll know you are doing all you can for your wine.

Where to put your wine rack

Most households do not have, or need, a special wine cellar but it is still worth paying attention to how your wine is stored and where you place your wine rack. If you always drink the wine within a few weeks of purchasing it, a small rack can be placed anywhere that isn't too hot or in bright light, but if you tend to keep even some of your bottles longer it is worth trying to achieve the best storage conditions you can.

Most homes have a few areas that will provide reasonable wine storage conditions. Possible spots include the area under the stairs, a hall cupboard, an unused fireplace or a basement. Rooms with fluctuating temperature, such as kitchens, are not suitable.

Table wines and ports should be stored lying down so that the cork remains moist. Only wines with metal caps are stored upright.

How wine ages

Each wine is meant to be drunk at a certain age, when its flavour will be fullest. Wine that hasn't reached this stage or is past its best will inevitably be a disappointment.

Storing conditions affect how quickly wine ages. Ageing should progress at a certain rate. If the conditions are not right, the wine will age too quickly, but premature ageing doesn't mean the wine is ready to drink sooner — it ruins it — and keeping a wine chilled below the optimum temperature prevents it ageing properly and reaching its full potential.

Temperature

Temperature is the most important factor when storing wine. A cool, stable temperature of 10–12°C (50–54°F) is best, although most wines can be stored between 5 and 18°C (41 and 64°F) without adverse effect. It is most damaging if the temperature fluctuates rapidly as this causes the wine to expand and contract, eventually damaging the cork.

Even wines meant to be drunk chilled should not be kept in the refrigerator for more than a few days.

Light

Light can increase the ageing process in wine and so wine should be kept in a dark place. Certainly avoid bright light, and don't store wine close to a window. Wine in light-coloured bottles is most affected, and sparkling wines are more susceptible than others.

Humidity

Moderate humidity is best for storing wine, for although the humidity will not affect the wine itself, too little (below about 50 per cent) will dry out the cork. High humidity is less damaging to the wine but it can cause the labels to rot and make it impossible to identify your wines.

Vibration

Some wine authorities believe wines are affected by vibration and so should be stored where they will not be disturbed or subjected to vibrations such as those caused by passing road traffic, low-flying planes or even very loud noises.

Odours

Wine can absorb odours through the cork so don't store it in a place where there are strong odours or food that may ferment.

Kitchen safety

Kitchen safety is largely a matter of commonsense:

- Carry plates to the pans rather than carry pans to the plates.
- Make sure hot and cold taps are clearly marked. Install a thermostatic mixer or tempering device, or turn the hot water down to 50°C (122°F) to help prevent scalds.
- Electrical outlets are best positioned away from the sink area. At least six electrical outlets are recommended for a kitchen, each placed on the wall, 25 cm (10 in) above the bench.
- Store fire control devices, such as a fire extinguisher and blanket, near the exit to the kitchen. Fit a smoke alarm near the entrance to the kitchen.

Child safety

Unless you are prepared to be extra careful, the best rule is to keep young children out of the kitchen. Gates or barriers like those used on stairways can be a handy way of blocking the entrance while allowing young children to see you. Carefully consider where to store or place the many dangerous items that are usually kept in the kitchen, and investigate the variety of inexpensive child-safe devices that make life easier — and safer — with a toddler.

- Use a safety gate at the entry point(s) to the kitchen to keep your child out of the danger zone, but still in your line of vision. Limit the entry points to the kitchen to one.
- Keep glassware in above-bench cupboards or shelves.
- Sharp knives should be stored in a wooden block or in sheaths, not loose in a drawer.
- Items with blades or sharp points — such as blender blades, skewers and corkscrews — should be kept well out of reach.
- Cleaning products, especially dishwashing machine detergent which is very corrosive, should be stored in a child-proof cupboard.

- Young children are insatiably curious. If they can't see what's on top of the stove, their natural instinct is to reach and grab! To prevent this disastrous scenario, fit a stove guard that blocks access to the front and both sides of the stove. If the stove top is part of a freestanding stove/oven unit, ensure that is anchored to the wall. Add an oven lock to prevent your child pulling open the oven door.

- Turn saucepan handles away from the stove front and use rear plates whenever possible.

- Ideally, the kitchen drawers should be located away from the stove and oven, and be fitted with safety latches or child-resistant locks.

- Cordless kettles mean one less cord to be able to pull; empty kettles are one less source of hot water.

Food poisoning

Hygiene in the kitchen is vital to avoid food poisoning. Raw and cooked food may contain organisms that will multiply and become dangerous if the food is not treated correctly. All cooking and storage should be done with this in mind. Hands, utensils and surfaces should be kept scrupulously clean and food should be stored in its appropriate place (such as the fridge). Generally, fruit and vegetables should be washed.

The more common types of food poisoning are due to salmonella, listeria and staphylococcus. Rarer forms include botulism and ciguatera.

Salmonella are a group of bacteria present mainly in meat, poultry and eggs. Salmonella, which causes upset stomachs and fever, is curable with antibiotics. It may, however, cause more severe reactions in pregnant women, babies or the elderly. Salmonella can be killed by boiling or heating food to very high temperatures.

Listeria is also a bacteria and is mainly found in soft cheese, pâté and ready-made food. Human immune systems cope well with it, but if listeriosis does occur, it can kill. It is of particular risk to pregnant women.

Staphylococcus are organisms that can cause food poisoning. They are found in prepared foods such as meat pies that are not stored properly.

They cause varying degrees of sickness but not fever and are untreatable. They cannot be killed by heating.

Botulism is a rare but virulent form of food poisoning caused by the toxins secreted by an anaerobic organism that can only grow in sealed cans and jars, or in the centre of cured meats where there is no oxygen present. Botulism does not cause immediate sickness but damages the nervous system and it often kills. Botulism can be killed by boiling for a short time. Preservatives inhibit botulism growth.

Ciguatera is a rare form of poisoning contracted by eating reef fish that have been eating toxic plankton. It affects the nervous system and often kills. It is not destroyed by cooking.

Fire drill

- Install a smoke detector. They are relatively inexpensive and very easy to install.

- Make sure every member of the household who is old enough to make a phone call knows the fire emergency number.

- Keep a fire blanket or a bucket of sand handy in case you need to smother a fire.

- Never leave a pan of oil unattended on the heat. If there is a fire in the frying pan, do not move the pan. Follow these steps:

  1. Turn off the heat if it is safe for you to do so.

  2. Smother the flames by covering the pan with a close-fitting lid, fire blanket, bucket of sand or damp cloth.

  3. Do not touch the pan for another 30 minutes.

- Never use water or an ordinary fire extinguisher to put out an oil fire.

HOMEMADE ANTISEPTIC
Here is a simple homemade recipe that can be used for minor cuts and grazes. Dissolve salt in boiled water. Dip a cotton wool ball in the warm, salty water and apply it to the injury.

FIRST AID FOR SCALDS

Here are some vital things to know about dealing with scalds.

Hot water still scalds 30 minutes after if has boiled, so make sure that hot water — whether it's in a cup, kettle or saucepan — is well out of reach of young children. If an accident does occur, follow these steps (every second counts!):

- Immediately cool the scalded skin either in or under cool, running tap water for at least 20 minutes.
- Always remove clothing as it holds the heat and can cause a deeper scald.
- Keep the child warm with a clean blanket and comfort him or her.
- Seek medical advice. Call an ambulance if the scald is serious.
- Do not use ice, oil or butter or anything else as these can damage the skin further.
- Do not touch the affected area or burst any blisters.
- Do not attempt to remove anything sticking to the burn.

Kitchen pests

Using toxic pesticides exposes not only you when you apply them, but also the whole household. Some groups of people are more prone to the side effects of pesticides: particularly vulnerable people include the elderly, children, babies, pregnant women, asthmatics and people with allergies. When used outside the home, pesticides may also kill beneficial insects and soil organisms in the garden. Many may also be toxic to birds, bees and fish.

Alternative methods of pest control focus on using mechanical means such as screens, traps and other practices that do not involve harsh chemicals. Often, prevention is a matter of commonsense, such as always putting away food in pest-proof containers and keeping your kitchen benches wiped clean.

As a last resort, some of the less toxic chemicals may be recommended.

Midnight munchers

Whether you're a human being or an insect, the best place for a midnight feast is the kitchen.

Grains and dried fruits, breakfast cereals, flour and spices are among the foods most vulnerable to pest attack in the pantry. Preventative measures are the most satisfactory: store these products in pest-proof jars and containers, bearing in mind that even the tiniest hole may be a large enough entry.

If you find an infested product, including eggs, dispose of it immediately in an outside bin.

If an infestation is bad, you may be tempted to treat cupboards and other hiding places. If you are prepared to give it a go and try a less toxic clean-up first, empty the cupboard, clear it of all food debris and wash it down with a detergent solution. If the infestation returns and you want to try something harsher, first clear and clean the cupboard, then dust the cracks and corners with diatomaceous earth (this may be available in food grade, suitable for use near food preparation areas). Alternatively, pyrethrins or neem (a tree which is native to western Asia) could be used.

The use of persistent surface sprays in food areas is not recommended.

Ants

It is possible to deter ants without using harmful pesticides.

- One of the simplest, least toxic ways to kill ants is to put 1 teaspoon liquid dishwashing detergent in a spray bottle of water and use the solution to spray trails of ants as they trek into your kitchen.

- Follow the trail of ants and try to locate the nest. Pour a cup of water into the nest and spray the ants with a spray containing pyrethrin as they emerge from the hole.

- Alternatively, place a few borax and sugar baits around the trail and nest.

- Every few days, until they disappear, puff pyrethrin-containing powder down the holes where ants enter the house.

Cockroaches

In theory, keeping the house clean — clearing away food scraps, grease and dust — helps keep cockroach populations down, but as they have a remarkable ability to live on a few crumbs at a time, in practice it can be difficult to control their numbers. Here are some tips to try:

- Cockroaches need somewhere to hide. Seal as many cracks and crevices as you can and use screens on windows and doors.
- Use sticky traps near breeding areas.
- Use low-toxicity baits such as 5 per cent borax and sugar in a small lid.
- Use pyrethrum sprays in crevices and harbouring areas.
- As a last resort use a pyrethroid spray such as permethrin, or a misting bomb containing permethrin and hydropene. This has the disadvantage of covering every surface. You need to leave the house for 2 hours at least, but a weekend would be even better.

Flies

Deter flies with some simple old-fashioned remedies.

- Make your own fly papers. Take equal volumes of sugar, corn syrup and water. Mix together and boil for 30 minutes. Spread the mixture on paper strips, and once they set to a sticky consistency, hang them near doors and windows.
- A pot-pourri mixture of dried orange and lemon peel and cloves stored in open jars is said to deter flies.
- Burn eucalyptus, lavender, citronella or peppermint essential oil in an oil burner.

Rats and mice

Traditional rat and mice poisons are effective but contain quite powerful poisons which can also kill pets and even children if accidentally ingested.

If you wish to avoid chemical baits, you can try a baited spring trap — rats love pumpkin or brazil nuts, while mice are partial to dried fruit. You should never handle a dead rat or mouse with your bare hands.

If you do opt for poison, multi-dose rodenticides are considered safest for both the environment and humans, in the case of accidental ingestion, but poisoned animals should be buried deep in the ground where they will not be eaten by other creatures.

Useful information

When you are following recipes in a cookbook, you may come across unfamiliar terms, or measurements that you need to convert. Following is a list of commonly used kitchen and cooking terms, as well as useful measurement conversions. (Note that the conversion tables shown are an approximation of conversions — in reality, 1 oz = 28.35 g, but it is easier to call it 30 g as scales do not measure small enough amounts to conveniently use any measurements of less than 1 g.)

Glossary of kitchen terms

Following is a useful list of cooking methods and other kitchen terms that are commonly used in recipes.

Absorption method To cook rice by adding the exact amount of water and cooking with the lid on until all the water is absorbed and steam holes appear in the surface of the rice.

Acidulate To add acid (such as lemon juice or vinegar) to cooking or soaking water to stop fruit or vegetables from oxidizing and discolouring.

Additive Something added to food to improve its keeping qualities, flavour, colour and texture. Often additives are listed by E numbers on packaging unless they are natural and not required to be listed by law.

Aerate To incorporate air into a mixture by sieving dry mixtures or whisking liquid mixtures (such as egg white or cream).

Al dente Italian phrase meaning 'to the tooth'. Refers to pasta and sometimes vegetables. The phrase means slightly underdone, so still with some 'bite'.

Weights

METRIC	IMPERIAL
10 g	¼ oz
15 g	½ oz
20 g	¾ oz
25/30 g	1 oz
55 g	2 oz
85 g	3 oz
115 g	4 oz (¼ lb)
140 g	5 oz
175 g	6 oz
200 g	7 oz
225 g	8 oz (½ lb)
250 g	9 oz
280 g	10 oz
310 g	11 oz
350 g	12 oz (¾ lb)
375 g	13 oz
400 g	14 oz
425 g	15 oz
450 g	16 oz (1 lb)
550 g	1 lb 4 oz
900 g	2 lb
1 kg	2 lb 4 oz
1.3 kg	3 lb
1.8 kg	4 lb

Liquid measures

ML	FL OZ	OTHER
5 ml		1 teaspoon
20 ml	½ fl oz	1 tablespoon*
40 ml	1¼ fl oz	2 tablespoons
60 ml	2 fl oz	3 tablespoons**
80 ml	2½ fl oz	⅓ cup ***
125 ml	4 fl oz	½ cup
150 ml	5 fl oz	
200 ml	7 fl oz	
250 ml	9 fl oz	1 cup
310 ml	10¾ fl oz	1¼ cups
330 ml	11¼ fl oz	1⅓ cups
375 ml	13 fl oz	1½ cups
400 ml	14 fl oz	
420 ml	14½ fl oz	1⅔ cups
435 ml	15¼ fl oz	1¾ cups
455 ml	16 fl oz	
500 ml	17 fl oz	2 cups
560 ml	19¼ fl oz	2¼ cups
1 litre	35 fl oz	4 cups

*The Australian tablespoon is 20 ml. The US and UK tablespoons are 15 ml, however this discrepancy should not affect most recipes.
**¼ cup
***4 tablespoons

Bain-marie Also called a 'water bath'. Usually a baking dish half-filled with water so delicate food is protected from direct heat. Often used for custards.

Bake blind To bake an empty pastry case before the filling is added. Ensures the pastry is cooked through and not soggy. Usually lined with baking paper and baking beads or rice or beans so it keeps its shape.

Bard To tie fat or fatty meat, such as bacon, over a lean joint or bird to stop it drying out as it cooks. The fat is removed before eating.

Oven temperatures

°C	°F	GAS MARK
70	150	¼
100	200	½
110	225	½
130	250	1
140	275	1
150	300	2
160	315	2–3
170	325	3
180	350	4
190	375	5
200	400	6
210	415	6–7
220	425	7
230	450	8
240	475	8
250	500	9

Baste To spoon or brush cooking juices or other fat over meat or other food during cooking.

Bind To use a liquid to make dry ingredients stick together and hold their shape.

Blanch To cook in boiling water for a few minutes and then refresh in cold water. This keeps colour in vegetables and loosens tomato and fruit skins. Also refers to potato chips that are precooked in hot fat before being fully cooked — this improves their texture and colour.

Blend To mix together well.

Bone To remove bones from a bird or piece of meat leaving the flesh intact.

Bouquet garni A small bunch of herbs used to flavour stocks, soups and stews. Removed before serving.

Braise To cook slowly on a bed of chopped vegetables and with a little liquid in a covered pan.

Brown To fry food (usually meat) quickly so the outside is cooked and has changed colour.

Bruise To squash slightly. Used for aromatics like lemongrass so they give out their flavour more easily.

Caramelize To heat food until the sugars on the surface break down and form a brown coating, which may be sweet or savoury.

Casserole To slowly cook a dish consisting of meat and/or vegetables on the stove or in the oven with a lid on tightly so that all the flavour and aroma is contained.

Clarify To skim or filter a liquid until it is clear, or to add beaten egg whites over heat, which then coagulate and trap any impurities.

Cream To beat butter or butter and sugar together until light and creamy.

Crimp To mark the edge of pastry or biscuits (cookies) or to seal two layers of pastry together in a scalloped pattern.

Croquette Mashed potato, minced (ground) meat, fish or vegetables, or any other similar mixture, made into a paste, then formed into log shapes, which are crumbed and fried.

Cube To chop food into even cubes. Usually bite-sized and for use in soups or stews so the size is not overly important.

Curdle Describes when a liquid separates, usually curds and whey for milk; when oil separates out of mayonnaise; or when egg separates from cake mixtures.

Cut in To mix hard fat with flour by cutting it in using two knives until it is chopped into small pieces, each coated in flour.

Deep-fry To fry something in oil, when the food is completely immersed in the oil.

Deglaze To loosen meat juices and flavours that may have stuck to the bottom of the pan when frying or roasting meat. A liquid is added to the hot pan and the pan is scraped and stirred. The liquid is then added to the dish or used to make gravy.

Degorge To salt something like eggplant (aubergine) in order to make it give up any bitter liquid, or to soak meat or fish in water to get rid of any impurities.

Devein To remove the dark vein-like digestive tracts from prawns (shrimp).

Dice To chop food into very small, even cubes.

Dot To scatter or put small pieces of butter over the surface of food before cooking.

Drain To remove liquid from food (usually with a colander or sieve). The food is kept and the liquid discarded unless specified.

Dredge To dust with a powder such as icing (confectioners') sugar or flour.

Drizzle To sprinkle liquid in a continuous stream.

Dry-fry To cook food in a frying pan without any fat.

Dry-roast To heat spices in a hot pan without oil to improve their flavour.

Dust To sprinkle lightly with a powder such as icing (confectioners') sugar or cocoa.

Escalope Very thin slice of meat, such as veal or chicken.

Fillet To cut meat from the bones.

Cup conversions

INGREDIENTS	CUP	METRIC	IMPERIAL
butter/margarine	1 cup	250 g	9 oz
tomatoes, chopped	1 cup	200 g	7 oz
white flour	1 cup	125 g	4½ oz
cooked long-grain rice	1 cup	185 g	6½ oz
uncooked long-grain rice	1 cup	200 g	7 oz
soft brown sugar	1 cup	185 g	6½ oz
white sugar	1 cup	220 g	7¾ oz
yoghurt	1 cup	250 g	9 oz

Cup measures are based on an Australian/UK cup (250 ml/9 fl oz). A US cup (235 ml/8 fl oz) may also be used in the same way without affecting most recipes.

Useful measures and approximate conversions

INGREDIENTS	TABLESPOONS	METRIC	IMPERIAL
breadcrumbs, dry	2 tablespoons	30 g	1 oz
cornflour (cornstarch)	1 tablespoon	30 g	1 oz
1 egg white	2 tablespoons	40 ml	1¼ fl oz
white flour	1 tablespoon	30 g	1 oz
powdered gelatine	4 teaspoons	15 g	½ oz
juice of 1 lemon	4 tablespoons	80 ml	2½ fl oz
juice of 1 lime	2 tablespoons	40 ml	1¼ fl oz
white sugar	1 tablespoon	30 g	1 oz

Fines herbes A mixture of finely chopped herbs, usually parsley, tarragon, chives and chervil.

Flambé To pour liqueur over food (usually in the pan, over heat) and set fire to it.

Flash point The point at which oil vapours will catch light but will not sustain burning. If oil gets this hot, it must be taken away from the source of heat immediately or it will reach fire point and burn.

Fold To mix one ingredient into another very gently (usually flour or egg whites) with a metal spoon or plastic spatula. The idea is to combine the mixture without losing the air. To fold properly, cut through the centre of the mixture, then run the edge of the spoon or spatula around the outer edge of the bowl, turning the bowl as you go.

French To trim the meat away from the bones of chops or ribs leaving the bone exposed.

Glaze A substance (often warmed jam or beaten egg) brushed over food to give it shine and colour.

Grease To lightly coat a pan or dish with oil or melted butter to prevent food sticking.

Hull To remove the stalks from berry fruit.

Infuse To flavour a liquid by heating it with aromatic ingredients (often spices) and leaving to let the flavour develop.

Julienne To cut into uniform thin matchsticks for quick cooking. Often used for stir-fries or in French cuisine.

Knead To stretch and fold dough to make it firm and smooth. This stretches the gluten in the flour and gives elasticity. Used for bread making but not for pastry making (over-handling will make pastry tough).

Knock back To knead gas bubbles out of a yeast-risen dough.

Knock up To separate the layers of puff pastry by running the back of the knife up the sides of the cut surface.

Lard To thread strips of lard through a lean piece of meat in order to baste it as it cooks.

Lardons Short strips of pork fat or bacon.

Liquidize To break down to a purée in a blender or food processor.

Macerate To soak food in a liquid so it absorbs the flavour of the liquid. Often used to describe soaking in alcohol and sugar syrup.

Marinate To tenderize and flavour food (usually meat) by leaving it in an acidulated seasoned liquid (a marinade).

Oven-fry To dip food in flour and then brush with hot fat before baking.

Pan-fry To fry in a frying pan in a small amount of fat.

Parboil To partially cook in boiling water before some other form of cooking. Most commonly used for roast potatoes which are parboiled before being added to the roasting meat.

Pinch A small amount of something — as much as can be held between your thumb and forefinger.

Pipe To force a mixture through a nozzle, either smooth or patterned, in order to cover or decorate a surface or make an exact shape.

Poach To cook food immersed in a gently simmering liquid.

Prove To allow a yeasted dough to rise; also to heat a frying pan or wok with oil or salt and then rub the surface, thus filling in any minute marks with the mixture and making it non-stick.

Punch down the dough A term used in bread making. A yeast dough which is left to rise is then punched with one firm blow of the fist, to remove the air from it.

Purée Food blended or processed to a pulp.

Reduce To boil or simmer liquid in an uncovered pan so that the liquid evaporates and the mixture becomes thicker and more concentrated in flavour. Most soups and stews are reduced — this should usually be done at a simmer so the flavour of the dish is not impaired by long, hard boiling.

Render To melt animal fat over low heat so that it separates out from any connective tissues. These go crispy and brown in the process. The fat is then strained to purify it.

Rest/relax To leave pastry in the fridge to allow the gluten, which will have been stretched during rolling, to contract again. Also means to leave batters until the starch cells in the flour have swelled through contact with the liquid; or to leave meat to let the juices settle back into the flesh before carving it.

Roast To cook in an oven at a high temperature without any covering in order to give a crisp, well-browned exterior and a just-cooked, moist interior. Usually applied to meat, poultry or vegetables.

Roux The basic mixture of many sauces — fat (usually melted butter) and flour. Used to thicken. Liquid is added to make a sauce.

Rub in To mix together flour and butter with your fingertips, usually for pastry. It will resemble fine breadcrumbs.

Scald To pour over or immerse in boiling water for a short time in order to cook only the outer layer. Also, to bring milk almost to the boil; or to sterilize kitchen equipment with boiling water.

Scallop A way of decorating pastry edges by pushing the edge in with one finger while pushing the pastry on both sides of that piece in the opposite direction using the other thumb and finger.

Score To ensure even cooking. Make incisions with a knife (usually into fish or meat) that do not cut all the way through.

Sear To brown the surface of meat in hot fat before fully cooking it.

Season To add flavour to something, usually salt and pepper, to bring out other flavours, or to smooth out the surface of a pan using hot oil or salt.

Shred To cut food into very thin strips.

Shuck To open bivalves such as oysters or to remove the husks, shells or pods from seeds.

Sift To shake dry ingredients (usually flour) through a sieve to aerate and remove lumps.

Simmer To cook liquid, or food in liquid, over low heat, below boiling point. The surface of the liquid will be moving with a few small bubbles.

Skim To remove fat or scum that comes to the surface of a liquid.

Slake To mix a powder, such as cornflour (cornstarch), with a little liquid to form a paste in order for it then to be mixed into a larger amount of liquid without forming lumps.

Soft peaks A term used when egg whites are whipped. The peak will fold over on itself when the beater is lifted.

Souse To pickle.

Steam To cook in the steam given off by boiling or simmering water.

Steep To infuse.

Stiff peaks A term used when egg whites are whipped. The peak will hold its shape when the beater is lifted.

Stir-fry To cook pieces of food quickly in a wok using only a little oil and moving them around constantly.

Strain To remove solids from a liquid by pouring through a sieve. The solids are discarded, unless specified.

Stud To insert flavourings such as whole cloves (into an onion) or slivers of garlic (into a piece of meat) into a piece of food at regular intervals.

Sweat To cook in fat over low heat without letting the food brown.

Tenderize To break down the tough fibres in flesh by mechanical (pounding), chemical (acid) or natural (hanging) means.

Toss To mix a dressing through food, usually a salad, so that it becomes coated. Also means to shake pieces of meat in flour to coat them; or to turn food in a pan by flipping it out of the pan, such as a pancake.

Trim To remove unwanted bits from meat or fish, or to cut something to a specific shape.

Truss To hold something, usually meat or poultry, in shape with string or skewers while it cooks.

Whip To incorporate air into something by beating it (cream, egg white) with a whisk or to form an emulsion by the same means (mayonnaise).

Whisk To beat rapidly with a wire whisk, to incorporate air and add volume.

Zest The coloured skin of citrus fruits. Avoid the bitter white pith below.

laundry

Managing the household laundry can be a daunting task — not surprising when you consider that the average person generates over a tonne of dirty clothes every year! Even with the ever-increasing sophistication of washing machines, dryers and irons, we all need some know-how to avoid those all-to-common disasters where our favourite item of clothing is shrunk beyond recognition, or sticks to the iron! Never again, though, as this chapter has everything you need to know about washing clothes, fabric care, drying clothes, ironing and pressing.

Energy-saving tips for the laundry

- **Water** Mainly cold water washing reduces both heating costs and energy consumption.

- **Soaking** Pre-soaking of heavily soiled or stained garments minimizes the need for hot water and harsh chemicals.

- **Washing machine** Full loads or half-load settings waste less water and detergent. Fast spin reduces drying time.

- **Detergent** Using concentrates reduces the amount of chemicals released into the environment; the correct dosage cuts out waste. Non-biological powder can be used if a household member has sensitive skin.

- **Clothes dryer** Clothes are hung and dried on a line outside whenever possible.

- **Stain-removal kit** Using a range of stain removers keeps clothes looking good and cuts down on dry-cleaning costs.

Fixing noisy water pipes

When you turn the tap off, and you hear a loud bang, or you hear a tapping sound while the water's running, this is probably due to water hammer, which is usually caused by poor installation of pipes. The only way you can fix this problem, without calling the plumber, is to try to isolate the rattling pipe and tighten it. If it's attached to the wall of your floor frame without enough fastenings it can rattle around when you turn your taps on and off.

1 Find the noise first. Get under the house and ask a helper to turn the taps on and off.

2 If the pipe is loose, saddle it to whatever you can — brickwork, bearer or joist — and once you've done that, simply flick the pipe with your finger and listen for any movement.

3 Keep applying the saddles on until the pipe is tightly in place. This may not solve the entire problem as there may be loose pipes you can't get to. If it's still a problem, call the plumber.

Checking for burst water pipes

If you have some damp in the walls or a wet spot in the garden, you may have a burst water pipe. To test for a burst pipe you can mark the meter and check it the next day.

1 Turn all your taps off tightly at night before you go to bed, and also turn off the toilets as they may have a tiny leak you can't see. You'll still be able to flush each toilet once during the night.

2 Go to your water meter and mark a line with felt tip pen on the glass covering the numbers. Match what you've done on a piece of paper.

3 Go to the meter again the next morning. Compare the position of the line on the meter with the one you copied onto paper the night before. If the line on the meter has moved since the night before, then you have a water leak. When you call the plumber you can at least avoid the lengthy inspection costs and, if possible, you can dig up and expose the burst pipe to save even more time and money.

Programming your wash

Washing machines are now very sophisticated. Many models have computerized controls, enabling you to program each load in specific ways. If you organize each washing load to make the most of this facility on your machine, you will save energy, and therefore money, each time you wash — for example, you should wash heavily soiled garments together in one load. Take these factors into consideration each time you sort out your washing:

- **Temperature** The hotter the water the greater its cleansing power, but you need to balance the temperature setting of your machine against the needs of each fabric type: only cotton and linen stand very hot temperatures, while silk may shrink and wool may felt. Hot water may result in a whiter wash, but it also uses more energy. To save energy, only use hot water for heavily soiled items. Alternatively, soak soiled items separately in a bowl of hot water before washing in a cooler load.

LINT TRAP
To prevent lint from washing water blocking your drains, fit the end of the water outlet with a section of pantihose (tights), and clean it regularly.

- **Wash time** Wash lightly soiled items and delicate fabrics, such as wool, for a shorter time. Dirty gardening gear, for example, may need longer.

- **Agitation strength** Regular agitation during the wash cycle may be too tough on lingerie or washable wool.

- **Load size** It is more energy-efficient to wash with the fullest load suitable for the fabric type. However, be careful not to overload the washing machine or the items will not move freely, making soil removal inefficient. Repeated overloading will also shorten the life of the machine itself. Use the half-load setting when washing small bundles of similar items; if you wash a small amount on the full-load setting, you'll waste a lot of water.

- **Spin cycle** For delicate fabrics, set the machine to a slower spin cycle and a shorter spinning time.

Essential oils in the home

Essential oils have a variety of uses in the home — not just in the laundry, but as disinfectants, fragrances, stain removers and insect repellents. Check the table opposite to see how you can put eucalyptus, lavender and pennyroyal oils to good use in your home.

Fabric care

Nowadays there is an enormous range of fabrics and finishes — both natural and synthetic — from which we can choose our clothes and other household textiles. To prolong their life and keep them looking in optimum condition, it's worth taking the time to discover what they're made from, and how they should be cared for.

Household uses for essential oils

ESSENTIAL OIL	PROBLEM	METHOD
Eucalyptus	Stains on clothing (e.g. perspiration marks, oil and soluble grease)	Add 2 teaspoons eucalyptus oil to a wash load or place an absorbent cloth under the stain. Moisten a clean rag with eucalyptus oil and gently but firmly brush the stain from its edge into the middle
	Stains on carpet	Put eucalyptus oil in a small spray atomizer and spray generously. Wipe with a clean absorbent cloth
	Ink (writing ink or printers' ink) on plastic or vinyl	Dip a cloth in eucalytpus oil. Test on a hidden patch first
	Glue, tar, chewing gum on fabric and other surfaces; adhesive tape on vinyl	Place a few drops on the stain, leave for 2 minutes and wash. Repeat a few times if necessary. Finish with a wipe of methylated spirits (denatured alcohol) and eucalyptus oil
	Washing bathroom	Kill bacteria by adding a couple of drops of eucalyptus oil to the final rinsing water
	Washing vinyl or lino flooring	Add 1 teaspoon eucalyptus oil to the washing water
Lavender	Washing bathroom	Kill germs by adding a couple of drops of lavender oil to the final rinsing water
	Washing clothes	Add fragrance to a washing load by adding a few drops of lavender oil to a face cloth and dropping it into the machine
	Mosquito bite	Apply undiluted to the bite
Pennyroyal	Flea repellent	Mix 18 drops undiluted pennyroyal oil with 500 g (1 lb 2 oz) bicarbonate of soda. Sprinkle over carpets and furniture, leave for one hour then vacuum
	For pets' bedding	Blend 20–30 drops pennyroyal oil with 2 teaspoons methylated spirits. Add to a pump spray bottle containing 2 cups water. Shake well then use on fine mist setting
	Fly repellent	Brush the oil onto woodwork surrounding doors and kitchen benches

ALLERGY ALERT IN THE LAUNDRY

Ingredients in detergents, fabric softeners and soaps can cause skin irritations and other allergic reactions. Some people are allergic to the solvent 1,1,1-trichloroethane, which is used in stain removers. It has a strong odour and can cause sneezing or a tightening of the chest in people with respiratory allergies.

If you or someone in your household is prone to allergies, take these precautions:

■ Consider using a non-biological detergent.

■ Rinse clothes extra carefully, perhaps by using the rinse cycle twice.

■ Before wearing new clothes wash them to remove excess factory finishes.

■ Wear gloves when hand-washing.

Sorting the washing

You can sort your washing in various ways. The obvious benefits of sorting are avoiding colour runs and saving on wear and tear, but it also makes your machine more energy efficient. How much time and trouble you take over it depends on the time you have available and your level of interest.

● **By fabric type** Fabric type determines the maximum temperature at which an article can be washed without causing damage. In some cases it also determines spin speed and washing machine cycle length. Consult the care label of the garment for information. If you wash all your clothes in cold water regardless of fabric type, you may simply need to separate woollens and other delicate items that you wish to wash by hand. It's usually best to separately wash items such as towels, especially new ones, to prevent lint spreading on to other garments.

● **By colour** Even when washing in cold water, you should separate loads of washing into coloureds and whites. You can break these groups down further into darks, mixed white and coloured patterns. Mainly white prints that are colourfast can be treated as 'white'. Always pay attention to the care label on each garment.

Instructions to 'wash separately' mean just that: excess dye may bleed out of the fabric for at least the first few washes.

- **By degree of soiling** Pull out the items that will benefit from pre-wash treatment, whether they are stained or heavily soiled. You should never wash a single very dirty item with a load of lightly soiled clothes.

While sorting the clothes for washing, attend to these small jobs at the same time:

- Empty pockets of paper tissues, coins, keys and any other items that could harm the washing machine or ruin the wash.

- Close buttons, zips and other fasteners to reduce the risk of your clothing tearing.

- Tie tapes and strings to prevent tangling in the wash.

- Brush clothes free of loose dirt and fluff.

- Mend any tears and holes to reduce the chance of holes enlarging during the washing process.

Care labels

Care labels on textiles usually refer to four different care processes: washing, bleaching, drying and ironing. They may also give dry-cleaning advice and information. Most instructions have fairly obvious meanings.

TESTING FOR COLOURFASTNESS

To test how fast a dye is — that is, how strongly it retains its colour — take these steps:

1 Dampen a piece of the hem or seam allowance or any part of the article that is not conspicuous.

2 Iron a piece of dry white fabric onto it.

3 If any colour transfers to the white piece, the dye is not colourfast. Wash the article separately in cool suds and rinse at once in cold water. Dry immediately.

Care labels give the consumer information on the best way to wash a particular item. They tend to err on the side of caution. Many silk items that are labelled 'dry-clean only' may in fact be carefully hand-washed. But if you do hand-wash an item with such a label, and something goes wrong, you cannot complain to the manufacturer.

When there's no care label, follow these guidelines:

- Synthetic fabrics in particular benefit from frequent washing as it prevents dirt from becoming absorbed into the fibres.

- To safeguard colour, finish and shape, and to minimize creasing, never wash hotter or longer, nor spin longer than recommended, unless you are absolutely confident of the results.

- Rinse thoroughly. Clothes and linen need at least two rinses to remove all traces of detergent and soil. Some finishes will not work effectively without proper rinsing — for example, shower-proofing may not work as well, and towelling may become scratchy.

- Blends are made by spinning together different fibres to form a yarn, which is then spun and woven or knitted. Mixture fabrics are made by weaving or knitting together yarns made from different fibres. When washing blends and mixtures, determine which fibre needs the gentlest treatment before you choose a washing method. For instance, wash a blend of polyester and wool as if it were all wool, in warm water.

A–Z fabric guide

Consult this alphabetical listing for some general information on the most popular fabric types.

Acetate

Acetate (also called cellulose acetate) is made from wood cellulose that is treated with acetic acid. Fabrics made from acetate are smooth and silk-like. Triacetate is more versatile and is made into a greater range of fabrics. Both acetate and triacetate are relatively weak and are easily abraded. Acetate fibres become even weaker when washed, so it is usually recommended that they be dry-cleaned. Triacetate can usually be machine-washed.

Guide to care symbols

SYMBOL	MEANING
⊻	Machine-washable (normal cycle)
⊻	Hand-wash only
△	Any bleach can be used
□	Tumble dry after washing
⊙	Tumble dry with high heat setting
⊙	Tumble dry with low heat setting
⟂	Hot iron
⟂	Medium iron
⟂	Cool iron
○	Dry-cleaning
Ⓐ	Any solvent
Ⓟ	Any solvent except trichloroethylene
Ⓕ	Petroleum solvent only

SCRATCHY LABELS

If your skin is irritated by a care label on your clothing detailing information you may need to refer to again, cut it off and reattach it to a side seam.

Both acetate and triacetate have little absorbency. They do not mildew and are generally not attacked by pests. They are damaged by concentrated acid or alkaline solutions and by solvents that contain acetone (such as nail polish remover and paint remover).

- Dry-clean if this is recommended on the care label.

- Wash gently if the care label recommends it.

- Use lukewarm water.

- Use mild soaps and detergents.

- Use household bleach cautiously for stains. Mineral spirits (also known as petroleum spirits) may also be used with care on acetate and triacetate. However, the fibres in acetate are damaged by solvents such as those used in perfumes and by others that contain acetone, such as nail polish remover.

- Roll in a towel to dry after hand-washing.

- Dry knits flat.

- Hang woven items to dry.

- Don't wring, twist or rub.

Acrylic

Acrylic (short for polyacrylonitrile) and modacrylic (modified acrylic) are both made from petroleum derivatives. They have soft, woolly, fluffy characteristics and are often used as a wool substitute. Modacrylics are also used in fake furs, as well as in children's nightwear — because of their flame resistance.

Cotton

Cotton is made from the fluffy fibres that surround the seed of the cotton plant. Its quality depends on the closeness and regularity of the weave, the construction of the fabric and the cotton plant itself. Generally, the longer the fibre (or staple), the better quality the cotton. Extra-long staples include Sea Island cotton, Pima cotton and Egyptian cotton.

Cotton is strong, absorbent and cool, and is particularly suitable for dyeing. It tends to wrinkle, but many cotton fabrics have been anti-wrinkle-treated,

YELLOWING COTTON
In most cases, ordinary bleach treatment will rid cotton of yellowing caused by age or excessive sunlight. If you have the facilities, you can try boiling the fabric for 45 minutes to an hour with detergent.

and also pre-shrunk. Cotton is prone to mildew if left wet and, like all cellulosic fibres, it is also prone to damage by acid, including the acid found in perspiration.

Linen

Linen is made from flax plant fibres, which consist of cellulose polymers. It is strong and durable, and can be put to use in a variety of different fabric types — damask, towels, bandages, sheets, lace, clothing and upholstery. Flax fibres are separated into long and short fibres by a process called hackling. Long fibres, or staple, are used for fine linen, while short staple, or tow, is used for functional items such as tea towels.

Flax fibres range in colour from pale yellow to dark brown. Linen is bleached, a process which weakens it, to produce white linen, or in preparation for dyeing. As the fibres are smooth, linen is fairly resistant to staining; it is also cool next to the skin and highly absorbent. Unless it has been pre-shrunk, linen will shrink a little the first time it is washed, and it is prone to heavy wrinkling; resin treatments, which also weaken the fibres, are sometimes applied to make linen less wrinkle-prone.

While some linen items are robust enough to bear tough laundering, even boiling, others, such as tailored jackets, are better off being dry-cleaned.

Nylon

Nylon is the name given to a group of polymers called polyamides derived from coal, petroleum, air, water and sometimes cereal waste products such as oat hulls or corn cobs. The characteristics of nylon fibres vary enormously and are sold under a variety of trade names. Generally, however, they are light, strong and highly resistant to abrasion. They are also highly elastic, and this is why they are such a suitable material for pantihose (tights). The fibres are wrinkle-resistant and have low absorbency. Nylon is not damaged by mildew, moths or other pests but it is prone to static build-up. It attracts dirt and holds oils.

- Wash white with white only as white nylon will pick up the slightest hint of colour in the washing water, rendering it dingy.

- Use a gentle machine cycle.

- Don't use chlorine bleach on nylon as it may yellow it. Use an oxygen bleach such as hydrogen peroxide instead.

Polyester
Polyester is produced from substances derived from coal, petroleum, air and water. A variety of polyester filaments are fabricated and these are made into a wide range of fabrics. Polyester is usually strong and wrinkle-resistant. It is not absorbent, it dries quickly, and although prone to oil stains, is otherwise stain resistant. Polyester fibres are not damaged by acids and alkalis, nor by mildew, moths or other pests. This fabric tends to retain body odours.

Rayon
Rayon is made from cellulose in either cotton or wood pulp and can be fabricated into a wide variety of materials. These include the following.

- **Viscose rayon** This constitutes the majority of rayon for sale, identified as 'viscose' or 'rayon'. It is soft and drapes well, with a feel a little like cotton. Highly absorbent but weaker than natural fibres, viscose rayon becomes weaker and prone to stretching when wet and tends to shrink on drying, so it needs gentle washing. It is prone to shrinking if not pretreated and may be wrinkle-prone, depending on how it was treated during manufacture. Viscose rayon mildews if left damp and is vulnerable to attack by silverfish but not moths.

- **Cuprammonium rayon** Also known as Bemberg or cupra rayon, this fabric is soft, lustrous and silky, and is used for linings, dresses and blouses, even flags.

- **High-Wet-Modulus rayons** These rayons have better wet strength and are often treated to avoid further shrinkage. They may look and feel like good-quality cotton and can usually be machine washed without trouble.

- **Lyocell** Sold under the trade name Tencel, and produced by dissolving wood pulp in a process considered environmentally favourable, lyocell is less prone to wrinkling and shrinking, and is stronger than viscose.

Some rayon is best dry-cleaned as the fibres weaken when wet and also often shrink. In addition, they can go limp and wrinkle after washing. Viscose rayon is often treated with water-soluble finishes and stiffeners that can dissolve in washing.

Silk

Silk, the epitome of luxury, is made from the filament secreted by the silkworm, the larva of the Chinese moth Bombyx mori, which feeds on the leaves of the mulberry tree. It is smooth, soft, lightweight, lustrous, strong and resilient. Although silk dyes brilliantly, it also abrades easily, making it a poor choice for upholstery. Silk is highly absorbent, partially wrinkle-resistant and prone to carpet beetles. Although it does not hold particles of dirt easily, because it is smooth, it does stain very easily.

- **Thrown silk** Fine and sheer fabrics such as georgette, taffeta, voile, crepe de Chine, organza and grenadine are made from thrown silk, whereby filaments from several cocoons are combined and wound onto a reel, then twisted into threads.

- **Spun silk** Short lengths of filament are carded, combed and spun into threads, which tend to become fuzzy over time.

- **Weighted silk** When the gum that covers the filament is boiled off, the fabric loses a lot of its weight. Manufacturers sometimes replace the lost weight with metallic salts, which add body but also weaken the silk.

- **Raw silk** Raw silk still contains the gum, so it is bumpy and irregular in texture.

Many care labels advise dry-cleaning silk because its fibres become weaker when wet and because it is prone to damage by alkalis. If in doubt, dry-clean — especially expensive silks, which may have special finishes you will never see again if you try washing them yourself. It is often possible to wash silks if you do it carefully, especially if they have been treated to make them washable. Some washable silks should not be dry-cleaned, so it is important to refer to care labels.

As with wool, hand-washing is the gentlest, safest option if you have decided to wash silk.

Velvet

Velvet is the name given to a type of fabric construction and not to the fibre it's made of. Velvet can be silk, cotton or an acetate/nylon blend. If the care instructions on a velvet garment are unclear, have it dry-cleaned.

Remove surface dust from soft furnishings upholstered in velvet with a vacuum cleaner or a soft brush.

Wool

The word 'wool' usually refers to sheep's wool, but can also mean the fibre that comes from the coats of Angora rabbits, cashmere goats, camel, alpaca, llama and vicuna. Wool is naturally warm, soft and absorbent. It provides cushioning and protects from dampness as it absorbs a great deal of moisture before becoming wet.

Wool fibres are used for a wide variety of textiles — woven clothing, knitting wool, upholstery and carpets. They vary in quality according to the type of sheep they come from — merino wool is the finest, softest and most elastic; Shetland and Botany wools are also good quality. The fleece type also varies: lamb's wool is the softest, while hogget wool

GIVE WOOL A REST

Because wool is elastic, experts recommend it be allowed to rest after wearing, washing and dry-cleaning. To rest a wool garment after you have worn it, follow these steps:

1 Empty the pockets, and do up any fasteners such as buttons and zips.

2 Brush the garment to protect it against moths.

3 Wipe it with a slightly damp, lint-free white cloth and air it. Airing reduces odours.

4 Hang it straight on a clothes hanger, then place it in the wardrobe.

comes from a yearling's first shearing and is also relatively soft compared to wool from more mature sheep.

Worsted yarns are made from long wool fibres that are spun to form a smooth, firm yarn. They make a flat, hard, smooth fabric commonly used in tailored suits. Fabrics made from worsted yarns are strong and relatively wrinkle-resistant but they can develop shiny patches.

Short wool fibres are used to make woollen yarns that spin into fuzzier yarns. They are warm but less durable than worsted, and are commonly used in jumpers and blankets.

Oiled wool fibres have not been stripped of as much of their natural lanolin as other wool fibres and are used for heavy jumpers.

Wool shrinks and is stain-resistant. You can often brush dust and dirt off the surface of wool; however, it can absorb and retain odours. Wool is highly vulnerable to moths but generally resists mildew unless it has been left damp for a long time.

Washing wool takes care as this fabric is prone to felting and shrinking: the fibres swell and weaken when wet. For this reason, many care labels advise dry-cleaning only. There's little doubt this is the best option for tailored items and bulky jumpers that are either difficult to dry or too special to risk spoiling.

With gentle treatment, however, many woollen items are fine to wash, and it certainly is cheaper than regular dry-cleaning. In fact, textile technology has developed to such a degree that manufacturers have come up with various chemical and physical processes which make wool more washable — for example, finishes such as Teflon protect knitted wool. Alkaline detergents should be avoided as they harm the wool fibres.

If washing by hand, follow these tips:

- Use cool, tepid or lukewarm water for a heavily soiled item.
- Use soap flakes or a detergent especially formulated for wool.
- If in doubt about whether a fabric is machine washable, hand-wash it.
- Gently squeeze the suds through the garment; rough agitation can damage the wool fibres.

STEAM TREATMENT
To smooth out a wrinkly wool garment, you can simply hang it up in a steamy bathroom.

- Rinse in cool clear water.
- Dry wool by wrapping it in a towel and rolling it gently. Never twist, pull or wring wool when it is wet. Dry it flat on a towel or other clean surface away from direct sunlight or heat.
- Don't soak a woollen garment for more than 5 minutes.

Where care labels advise it, or when you are prepared to risk it, woollens can be machine washed on a gentle cycle. Your washing machine may even have a special 'wool' cycle.

- Use cool or lukewarm water.
- Use a gentle detergent suitable for wool.
- Use a fast spin to ensure the item is as dry as possible.
- Dry it flat.
- Don't tumble dry unless the care label advises it.

Washing guidelines

A whiter wash

Are your whites grey? Do some of your clothes have persistent grease spots you can't remove? You could try some old-fashioned whitening methods, such as these. Check the table on pages 182–89 for special instructions for individual fabric types.

- **Blue** Washing blue, made from the pigment indigo, counteracts the yellow tint that results from perspiration and the use of soap and soda.
- **Methylated spirits (denatured alcohol) and cloudy ammonia** Adding 1 cup of each to the washing water every so often helps to keep whites actually looking white.

FIRE RISKS

- Synthetic fibres such as nylon and polyester may be slow to ignite, but eventually they will burn and melt at a very high temperature.

- Light materials such as voile and muslin burn faster than the heavy types of fabric used in curtains.

- Fabrics that are mixed from synthetic material and cellulose have a wicking effect as the cellulose acts as a wick onto which the synthetic polymer fibres melt.

- Wool and silk readily char and do not spread the flame.

- Raised pile fabrics are more of a fire hazard as they have a greater surface area in contact with air.

- Cellulosic fabrics readily burn and also produce flammable gases.

- **Borax** Add ½ cup borax to a machine wash. This is particularly effective if you dry the items in the sun after washing.

- **Sunlight** If you leave cloth in strong sunlight for a day, the sun plus oxygen and moisture from the air create a slow bleaching effect.

- **Frost** Bleaching also occurs when damp clothes become iced over. However, frost also weakens fabric, so handle items with care. To prevent tears, wipe the clothesline with boiling water and salt before you peg the clothes out in the first place. Ideally, wait until the washing has thawed before bringing it in.

KEEP YOUR MACHINE CLEAN
Many manufacturers recommend running a washing machine through a complete cycle with neither powder nor clothes in it every month or so. This will keep the machine clean and free from deposits.

Fabrics and their washing requirements

FABRIC	DESCRIPTION	SPECIAL REQUIREMENTS
Acetate	Widely used cellulose derived fabric	Wash gently in lukewarm water. Handle gently when wet. Take care with stain solvents
Acrylic	Synthetic fibre that does not shrink	Treat heavy knitted articles with care to avoid stretching. Gentle machine or hand-wash, inside out to prevent pilling. Use fabric softener regularly to reduce static electricity. Use a low tumble dryer setting; dry knits flat
Angora	Fluffy fibre from the Angora rabbit	Hand-wash with care. To dry, lay flat away from direct sun or heat. Brush with teasel brush (a spiky brush) when dry to raise the surface
Cashmere	Natural fibre from the downy undercoat of the Tibetan cashmere goat	Hand-wash with care. Will quickly felt if washed too vigorously. To dry, roll in a dry towel, press to remove excess water, then repeat with a second towel. Finally, lay flat to dry on a fresh towel
Clydella	Mixture fabric of natural fibres, wool and cotton	Do not rub
Corduroy	Cut weft pile fabric with corded effect, usually cotton	Wash deep and bright colours separately
Cotton	Strong natural fibre which can withstand vigorous washing	Machine-wash if you wish but be more cautious with loose weaves, trims and linings. Bleach when desired but rinse well afterwards. Dry in the sunlight for a lightening effect. Don't leave out in the sun for more than a few hours or it will yellow
Cotton (drip-dry)	Cotton with special finish for crease resistance and minimum iron	Machine-wash
Denim	Twill weave, usually cotton or cotton blend	Allow for shrinkage. Not all denim is colourfast
Dylan	Shrink-resistant wool	Sometimes machine-washable. Normal rinse. Normal spin, do not wring
Egyptian cotton	Fine-quality natural cotton fibre in closely woven cloth	Machine-wash
Elastane fibres	Synthetic stretch fibres	Wash according to other fibres in fabric and not above 50°C (122°F)

MAX. WASH TEMP.	AGITATION	RINSE	SPIN	IRONING NOTES
40°C (104°F)	Gentle	Cold	Short	Damp iron on wrong side with cool iron
40°C (104°F)	Minimum	Cold	Short	Cool iron if required
40°C (104°F)	Minimum	Warm	Short	If desired, warm iron over damp cloth, or use steam iron
40°C (104°F)	Gentle; do not wring or twist	Cold	Do not spin	Press on wrong side with warm iron under damp cloth, or use steam iron
40°C (104°F)	Minimum	Normal	Normal; do not hand wring	If required, warm iron on wrong side when damp
50°C (122°F)	Medium	Cold	Drip-dry	Do not iron. Remove creases by steaming
95°C (203°F) whites 60°C (140°F) coloureds	Maximum	Normal	Normal	If required, warm to hot iron when dry
50°C (122°F)	Medium	Cold	Drip-dry	Warm to hot iron when dry if required
95°C (203°F) whites 40°C (104°F) coloureds	Maximum	Normal	Normal	Hot iron when damp
40°C (104°F)	Minimum; do not rub	Normal	Normal; do not wring	Warm iron over damp cloth, or steam iron
95°C (203°F) whites 60°C (140°F) coloureds	Maximum	Normal	Normal	Hot iron on wrong side when damp
50°C (122°F)	Medium	Cold	Short spin or drip-dry	Do not iron

Fabrics and their washing requirements

FABRIC	DESCRIPTION	SPECIAL REQUIREMENTS
Fibreglass fabric	Woven from fine glass filaments. Flame-proof and resistant to bacteria	Handle gently; liable to fray if machine-washed. Abrasion can cause damage to the surface and loss of colour
Flame-retardant fabrics	Various fabrics designed to increase flammability	Do not soak, bleach or boil
Flame-retardant finishes	Various fabric finishes designed to decrease flammability	Do not use soaps or soap products. Medium agitation. Rinse carefully with cold water. Do not soak or bleach.
Foam backs	Fabrics to which a layer of polyurethane or polyester foam has been bonded to the back of the face fabric to give warmth without weight and to preserve shape	Not all foam backs are suitable for home washing. If in doubt dry-clean. Otherwise proceed as for face fabric
Glazed cotton	Cotton with special finish. Only permanently glazed cotton will retain sheen on washing	No special requirements
Helenca	Process which gives high stretch to yarns such as nylon and polyester	No special requirements
Lamb's wool	Natural fibre, fine-graded, high-quality wool	Hand-wash with care
Laminates	Two or more layers of fabrics bonded together	Not all are suitable for home washing. If in doubt dry-clean. Washable laminates should be laundered according to face fabrics
Lastex	Natural stretch yarn made from extruded rubber (latex)	If no advice on label, proceed at your own risk
Linen	Natural fibre made from flax	Wash at high temperatures. Can bleach and boil if white
Linen (delicate)	Lace or fine linen blouses	Hand-wash or place item in old pillowcase before washing on gentle setting. Use mild detergent; avoid one with optical brighteners which can cause white spotting

MAX. WASH TEMP.	AGITATION	RINSE	SPIN	IRONING NOTES
40°C (104°F)	Gentle	Cold	Drip-dry	Do not iron
40°C (104°F)	Minimum	Cold	Short spin	Press lightly with a cool iron on wrong side while slightly damp
50°C (122°F)	Medium	Cold	Short spin or drip-dry	Cool iron
As for face fabric	As for face fabric	As for face fabric	As for face fabric	Iron according to face fabric
50°C (122°F)	Medium	Cold	Short spin or drip-dry	Hot iron on wrong side when damp. Finish by polishing on right side
60°C (140°F) white nylon 50°C (122°F) other	Medium	Cold	Short spin or drip-dry	Warm iron when dry if necessary
40°C (104°F)	Gentle	Cold	Roll in towel, then dry flat	Press lightly with warm iron under damp cloth or use steam iron. Brush up pile when dry
As face fabric	As face fabric	As face fabric	As face fabric	Iron if necessary according to face fabric
30°C (86°F)	Gentle	Cold	Short	Do not iron
95°C (203°F) whites 60°C (140°F) coloureds	Maximum	Normal	Normal	Hot iron when damp
40°C (104°F)	Do not wring	Normal	Roll in a towel to remove excess moisture then dry flat away from direct source of heat	Iron when still damp

Fabrics and their washing requirements

FABRIC	DESCRIPTION	SPECIAL REQUIREMENTS
Linen (sturdy)	Tablecloths, sheets, woven towels	Presoak overnight to remove stubborn stains. If tumble drying, remove while still damp to prevent overdrying which can make linen brittle
Lurex	Specially processed metallic thread incorporated into other fabric	Wash according to fabric type
Minimum iron	Easy-care finish	Wash according to fabric type
Modal	Viscose in modified form with improved wet strength	No special requirements
Mohair	Natural fibre from the Angora goat	Hand-wash only
Nylon	Strong versatile synthetic fibre	No special requirements
Permanent press	Technique for giving permanent shape and creases to garments	Wash according to fabric type
Polyester	Very strong synthetic fibre	Wash regularly as attracts greasy soiling. Pre-treat greasy stains. Wash inside out to prevent pilling
Polyester cotton	Blend	Do not allow to become heavily soiled before washing
Proban	Flame-retardant finish	Do not use soap
PVC	Synthetic thermo plastic fibre	Shrinks over 70°C (158°F). Coats and raincoats: sponge only
Rayon	Read care label carefully as finishes and manufacturing processes are so varied. Specific care labels may recommend more vigorous handling	Either hand-wash or use machine's gentle cycle if care label recommends machine washing. Use a mild, non-alkaline detergent. Dry knits flat; hang woven items
Rigmel	Shrink-resistant finish for cotton	No special requirements
Sanforized	Shrink-resistant finish	Wash according to fabric type

MAX. WASH TEMP.	AGITATION	RINSE	SPIN	IRONING NOTES
50°C (122°F)	Minimum	Extra rinse	Fast; don't wring	Iron when still damp
As fabric type	As fabric type	As fabric type	As fabric type	Warm iron
40–50°C (104–122°F)	Minimum	Cold	Drip-dry	Warm iron if necessary when dry
40–60°C (104–140°F)	Maximum	Normal	Normal	Hot iron when damp. If necessary warm iron for polyester blends
40°C (104°F)	Gentle	Cold	Roll in towel, then dry flat	Press on wrong side under damp cloth with warm iron or use a steam iron. Brush up pile when dry
60°C (140°F) whites 50°C (122°F) coloureds	Medium	Cold	Short spin or drip-dry	If necessary, cool iron when dry
As fabric type	As fabric type	As fabric type	Do not wring	Not necessary
50°C (122°F)	Medium	Cold	Short spin or drip-dry	If necessary, cool iron when dry
60°C (140°F) whites 50°C (122°F) coloureds	Medium	Cold	Short spin or drip-dry	If necessary, warm iron when dry
50°C (122°F)	Medium	Cold	Short spin or drip-dry	Cool iron
40°C (104°F)	Minimum	Cold	Short spin	Do not iron
30–40°C (86–104°F)	Gentle	Cold	Squeeze rather than wring	If in doubt, cool iron
95°C (203°F) whites 60°C (140°F) coloureds	Maximum	Normal	Normal	Hot iron when damp
As fabric type	As fabric type	As fabric type	As fabric type	Iron according to fabric type

Fabrics and their washing requirements

FABRIC	DESCRIPTION	SPECIAL REQUIREMENTS
Sarille	Modified viscose with wool-like qualities	No special requirements
Scotchguard	Water- and oil-repellent finish	Wash according to fabric type. Rinse thoroughly
Silk and wild silk	Natural protein fibre made by silkworms	Use mild soap or detergent. Regular laundry detergent is alkaline and could damage silk fibres. Don't use chlorine bleach; use hydrogen peroxide or sodium perborate bleaches. Rinse thoroughly, dry gently. Don't soak for long periods
Triacetate	Synthetic cellulose-derived fibre	More robust in wash and wear than acetate
Viloft	Tubular viscose fibre with high bulk and extra absorbency	Washes well often
Viscose	Widely used cellulose fibre used on its own and in blends	No special requirements
Viyella	55% lamb's wool, 45% cotton	Treat gently
Wool	Natural sheep fibre available in many qualities	Hand-wash unless specifically advised to machine wash
Wool (machine washable)	Process which makes wool shrink resistant	Do not wring

Hand-washing

Hand-washing is still desirable for many items, such as woolly jumpers or delicate lingerie. For the best results, follow these steps:

1 Fully dissolve the granules of powder in the water.

2 Soak to loosen dirt but take care never to soak wool.

3 Agitate by picking up and dropping clothes in the water, or by kneading them gently.

4 Rinse clothes thoroughly.

5 Drip-dry clothes if you have the space, or roll them in a towel to remove moisture, then hang them up to dry.

MAX. WASH TEMP.	AGITATION	RINSE	SPIN	IRONING NOTES
40°C (104°F)	Normal	Normal	Normal	Hot iron when slightly and evenly damp
As fabric type	As fabric type	As fabric type	Drip-dry	Warm iron if necessary
30–40°C (86–104°F)	Minimum	Cold	Short spin, do not hand-wring	Warm iron when slightly and evenly damp. Cool iron wild silk
40°C (104°F)	Minimum	Cold	Short spin	Cool iron when damp
50°C (122°F)	Medium	Cold	Short spin or dry	Not usually necessary
60°C (140°F)	Maximum	Normal	Normal	Hot iron on wrong side when damp
40°C (104°F)	Minimum do not rub	Normal	Normal spin; do not hand-wring	Warm iron on wrong side while slightly damp
40°C (104°F)	Minimum do not rub	Normal	Normal spin; do not hand-wring	Warm iron under damp cloth, or steam iron
40°C (104°F)	Minimum do not rub	Normal	Normal spin; do not hand-wring	Warm iron over a damp cloth, or use a steam iron

Soaking success

Heavily soiled or stained articles may need soaking before washing. When soaking coloured items, follow this check list:

- Check that the dye can withstand soaking (if in doubt, do not soak).
- Fully dissolve the washing powder (there may be spotting if concentrated powder is left in contact with the fabric).
- Select a water temperature that is not too hot for the fabric type.
- Make sure the article is not bunched up.
- Soak white and coloured articles separately.

Removal of washable stains

TYPE OF STAIN	REMOVAL METHOD
Excess liquid	Blot excess liquid with a dry cloth or paper towel before soaking
Food solids	Scrape off solids such as cooked egg before soaking
Fresh stains	Soak in cold suds for 30 minutes to prevent the stain from setting in the fabric, then wash normally
Dried stains	Lubricate with glycerine by applying a mixture of 1 part glycerine to 2 parts water to the stain. Leave for 10 minutes then treat as a fresh stain
Residual marks on white fabric	Bleach with a solution of hydrogen peroxide (1 part '20 white fabric volume' hydrogen peroxide to 9 parts water). Leave to soak for 1 hour, then wash as usual

Stain removal

When dealing with stains on fabric, the golden rule is this: act fast. A speedy response may prevent a stain from setting and allow you to use a milder remedy. Some delicate fabrics may withstand methods that are appropriate for removing a fresh stain, but the same fabrics may be damaged by the harsher methods necessary for attacking set stains. If you leave the wrong stain to set on the wrong fabric, you could end up with permanent stains — synthetic and drip-dry fabrics are more prone to this than natural fibres.

Here are some general guidelines for stain removal:

- **Remove the spill first** Mop liquid spills on washable fabrics with a cloth and remove solids with the back of a knife.

- **Never rub a stain** Rubbing only pushes the stain further into the fabric. Instead, use a pinching action with a clean cloth or a paper tissue to remove as much of the staining substance as possible.

- **Outside in** When working with solvents on a stain, always work from the outer rim of the stain to minimize its spread.

● **Test first** If possible, first test a stain remover, especially a solvent, on a hidden or less conspicuous area of a garment, such as the hem or seam allowance. (See 'Testing for colourfastness', page 171.)

Absorbent pad method of stain removal

For treating and washing stains, use the absorbent pad method. This requires two pads of cotton wool or something similar.

1 Soak one pad in the appropriate solvent.

2 With the solvent pad under the stain and the other pad on top, dab the stain.

3 When some of the stain has transferred to the top pad, turn it over so its clean side is in contact with the fabric and repeat.

4 Change the top pad and continue working until no stain comes through.

5 Wash as usual.

THE ESSENTIAL STAIN-REMOVAL KIT

Keeping a household stain-removal kit in your laundry gives you a head start on stains. A basic kit should contain the following items, but take care with solvents and only use them if they are really necessary.

■ Acetone or amyl acetate, solvents found in nail polish remover

■ Bicarbonate of soda

■ Blotting paper

■ Borax

■ Clothes brush

■ Cotton wool, paper tissues, clean dry rags

■ Cream of tartar

■ Droppers

■ Dry-cleaning fluid

■ Eucalyptus oil

■ Glycerine for lubrication

■ Household ammonia

■ Hydrogen peroxide

■ Kerosene

■ Lemon juice

■ Methylated spirits

■ Potassium permanganate

■ Precipitated chalk

■ Proprietary grease

■ Salt

■ Scraper

■ Turpentine

■ White vinegar

Stain removal

TYPE OF STAIN	SOLVENT	METHOD
Ballpoint ink	Methylated spirits	Absorbent pad method (see pg 191)
Bicycle oil	Proprietary grease solvent	Absorbent pad method
Black lead	Proprietary grease solvent	Absorbent pad method
Chalks and crayons	Detergent Use methylated spirits for stubborn marks Wash as normal	Brush off as much as possible while dry. Brush stained area with suds (1 dessertspoon to 2 cups water)
Chewing gum	Methylated spirits Ice cube	Absorbent pad Rub the gum with an ice cube to harden it. You may be able to pick it off by hand, then wash as usual to remove any traces
Cod liver oil, cooking fat and heavy grease stains	Proprietary grease solvent	Absorbent pad method
Contact adhesives	Amyl acetate	Absorbent pad method
Dried fruit stain (for all but very delicate fabrics)	Boiling water	Stretch the fabric over a basin. Pour over almost boiling water
Dried fruit stain (very delicate fabric)	Lemon juice	Spread the fabric over blotting paper and sponge on the wrong side with hot water. If the mark remains, moisten with a little lemon juice and rinse with hot water
Felt pen ink	Soap Methylated spirits	Use hard soap to lubricate the stain. Wash as normal. For obstinate stains use methylated spirits and the absorbent pad method. Wash again to remove final traces
Fresh fruit stain	Salt	Before it has had time to dry, cover the stain in salt and wash without a soap (the alkali in the soap fixes rather than fades the stain)

TYPE OF STAIN	SOLVENT	METHOD
Glue, tar, chewing gum on fabric and other surfaces; adhesive tape on vinyl	Eucalyptus oil	Place a few drops on the stain, leave for 2 minutes and wash. Repeat a few times if necessary. Finish with a wipe of methylated spirits and eucalyptus oil
Grass stain	Methylated spirits, cream of tartar	If the fabric is too delicate to wash, daub with methylated spirits on a clean cloth. If it can be laundered, soak in cold water then cover with a little cream of tartar and leave it in the sun
Hair lacquer	Amyl acetate	Absorbent pad method
Ink stain on coloured fabric	Milk, tomato	Soak the stained part immediately in slightly warm milk. Rinse. Or rub the stain with half a ripe tomato, then soak the fabric in cold water. The stain should disappear in the next laundering
Ink stain on white fabric	Salt, lemon	Sprinkle with salt immediately then rub with a cut lemon. Rinse and wash off
Iron mould on white cotton and linen only	Oxalic acid solution	Dissolve ½ teaspoon oxalic acid crystals in 1 cup hot water. Tie a piece of cotton tightly around the edges of the stained area to prevent the solution spreading and immerse the stained part. Leave for 2–3 minutes. Rinse thoroughly and wash in rich suds
Iron mould (rust marks) on wool, synthetic fabrics and all delicate fibres	Lemon juice	Flood the stain with lemon juice and leave for 10–15 minutes. Place a damp cloth over the stain and iron. Repeat several times as necessary. Rinse and wash as usual
Lipstick and blusher	Proprietary grease solvent	Soak light stains then wash in the usual way. For heavier stains, use the absorbent pad method

Stain removal

TYPE OF STAIN	SOLVENT	METHOD
Lipstick alternative on washable fabrics	Kerosene	Sponge
Lipstick on non-washable fabric	Methylated spirits or eucalyptus oil	Absorbent pad method
Marking ink	Marking ink eradicator	Follow manufacturer's instructions
Metal polish	Proprietary grease solvent	Absorbent pad method
Mildew on coloured articles	Detergent	Regular soaking followed by washing in rich suds. If the stain is not entirely removed, it may gradually fade with subsequent washes
Mildew on linen or cotton	Precipitated chalk	Wet the mildewed parts, rub with ordinary laundry soap, cover with precipitated chalk and rub it in. Leave for at least 1 hour then rinse. Repeat if necessary
Mildew on white cottons and linens without special finishes	Household bleach and vinegar	Soak in 1 part bleach to 100 parts water with 1 tablespoon vinegar. Rinse thoroughly then wash
Mildew on white drip-dry fabrics	Hydrogen peroxide solution	Soak in 1 part hydrogen peroxide ('20 volume') and 9 parts water until stain has gone. Rinse thoroughly and wash as normal
Mildew (old and persistent stain)	Potassium permanganate	Try soaking item in solution of 1 teaspoon potassium permanganate in 2 cups water
Mildew (set in)	Salt	Rub the stain with damp salt and expose to warm sunshine if possible
Mildew (slight stain)	Lemon juice	Sponge with lemon juice and place in the sun until the spores have disappeared (about 1 day)
Nail polish	Amyl acetate	Absorbent pad method
Nicotine	Methylated spirits	Absorbent pad method

TYPE OF STAIN	SOLVENT	METHOD
Paint (oil-based)	Turpentine or amyl acetate	Absorbent pad method
Paint (water-based)	Water	Sponge paint splashes immediately with cold water. Dried paint is permanent
Permanent ink	Oxalic acid solution (suitable for linens and white cottons only)	Dissolve ½ teaspoon oxalic acid crystals in 1 cup hot water. Tie a piece of cotton tightly round the stained area to prevent the solution spreading and immerse the stained part. Leave for 2–3 minutes. Rinse thoroughly and wash in rich suds
Perspiration (fresh)	Ammonia	Dampen with water then hold over an open bottle of household ammonia
Perspiration (old stains)	White vinegar	Sponge with white vinegar, rinse thoroughly then wash as usual
Perspiration (on wool)	Lemon juice	Sponge with a 1:1 solution of lemon juice and water then hang up to air
Plasticine	Proprietary grease solvent or mineral spirits	Scrape or brush off as much as possible. Apply solvent using the absorbent pad method then wash to remove final traces
Scorch marks (light)	Glycerine	First try soaking in cold water and soap or detergent suds, then wash. If stain persists, moisten with water and rub glycerine into the stain. Wash. Try removing residual marks by soaking in a hydrogen peroxide solution. Heavy scorch marks that have damaged the fabric fibre normally cannot be removed. Alternative method: dampen the affected area and leave in the sunlight for a few hours. Soak a piece of linen in a solution of 3% hydrogen peroxide, place it over the scorch then press with a hot iron. (Test for colourfastness first)

Stain removal

TYPE OF STAIN	SOLVENT	METHOD
Shoe polish	Glycerine and proprietary grease solvent	Lubricate stain with glycerine then use solvent and absorbent pad method. Wash to remove final traces
Sour milk	Laundry detergent and cloudy ammonia	Rinse in cold water, then soak for 30 minutes in laundry detergent and lukewarm water with 1 teaspoon cloudy ammonia. Rinse and wash in lukewarm water
Stains on clothing (perspiration marks, oil and soluble grease)	Eucalyptus oil	Add 2 teaspoons eucalyptus oil to a wash load. Place an absorbent cloth under the stain. Moisten a clean rag with with eucalyptus oil and gently but firmly brush the stain from its edge into the middle
Sunscreen	Proprietary grease solvent	Absorbent pad method
Tar	Eucalyptus oil, proprietary grease solvent, benzine or lighter fuel	Scrape off surplus. Apply solvent using the absorbent pad method. Rinse and wash off as soon as possible
Verdigris (green stains from copper pipes) on wool, synthetic fabrics and all delicate fibres	Lemon juice	Flood the stain with lemon juice and leave for 10–15 minutes. Place a damp cloth over the stain and iron. Repeat several times if required. Rinse and wash as usual
Verdigris on white cotton and linen only	Oxalic acid solution	Dissolve ½ teaspoon oxalic acid crystals in 1 cup hot water. Tie a piece of cotton tightly round the stained area to prevent the solution spreading and immerse the stained part. Leave for 2–3 minutes. Rinse thoroughly and wash in rich suds

Special washing tasks

Following is a special guide for tackling some of those difficult washing tasks around the home.

Doonas and eiderdowns

Dry-cleaning is usually the recommended option for doonas (duvets) and eiderdowns, but if you have the space to tackle them at home, use warm, soapy water and knead to aid cleaning. Rinse well in several changes of water. Do not wring or spin dry the doona, just squeeze out as much water as possible, then place it flat on grass, if you can, on an old sheet. Turn it over and shake it from time to time. When it is absolutely dry, shake it thoroughly and hang it on the line, then beat it gently to separate the filling.

Blankets

Don't wash a woollen blanket in hot water as it will felt (that is, it will become matted in texture). You should use warm water instead with a mild detergent and a gentle washing action. Do not leave a woollen blanket to soak for more than 5 minutes. A cup of ammonia will help to soften the fabric. Spin dry, shake vigorously and reshape it before hanging it on the line to dry.

Non-woollen blankets are invariably machine washable. If yours is heavily soiled, it's a good idea to soak it for about 20 minutes first. Then wash it on a gentle cycle in the washing machine in warm water, followed by a cold rinse and a fast spin dry. Hang the blanket out to dry on a line and, if possible, spread the weight of the blanket over two lines. Alternatively, lay it flat on an old sheet on the grass.

Curtains

Many types of curtains are washable, especially if you wash them by hand. Take the curtains outside and shake them first to get rid of as much dust as possible. If you are washing new curtains for the first time, you should soak them overnight in salty water to remove fabric dressings (finishing treatments).

HOME DRY-CLEANING KITS

Instead of sending your delicate clothes to the dry-cleaner, you can try freshening them in the tumble dryer by using a kit comprising stain removers, a dry-cleaning sheet and a dryer-safe plastic bag. These kits are good at removing odours such as stale cigarette smoke and cooking smells but they don't clean as well as the professionals. They do, however, help minimize the number of visits to the dry-cleaners. They also use chemicals that, while not considered 100 per cent environmentally friendly, are less harmful to the environment than 'perc'.

Pillows

It is possible to wash feather-filled pillows, but take care not to strip the feathers of their natural oils. Follow these steps:

1 Use a mild detergent or soap and wash them either by hand or in a front-loading machine. (A top loader may be too rough.)

2 Rinse the pillows thoroughly and, if washing by hand, squeeze out any excess water.

3 Otherwise spin dry in any type of washing machine.

4 Do not hang up pillows to dry as the filling will fall to one end. If you don't have a dryer, lay them flat. If you're drying them in a tumble dryer, use a low temperature. A couple of towels in the dryer will speed up the drying time, and two or three tennis balls will help to break up clumps of feathers. Make sure the pillows are completely dry before putting them away.

Gloves

How you clean gloves depends on the material.

Leather gloves

As a rule, you should not wash suede and lined leather gloves, but some leather gloves are washable. If you want to try washing leather gloves, follow these steps:

1 Empty the fingers of dust and lint.

2 Wash the gloves in warm water and mild soap suds.

3 Squeeze gently.

4 Rub extra soap on any stained patches.

5 Turn the gloves inside out and repeat the gentle squeezing.

6 Rinse the inside, then the outside.

7 Dry the gloves flat, working them several times with your hands as they dry to prevent them from stiffening. When they are half dry, put the gloves on to shape them.

8 When they are completely dry, rub them with a little leather conditioner. If they do dry stiff, wet them a little and work them with your hands to soften them.

Woollen gloves

Wash woolly gloves by hand as they may pull apart in a machine wash.

1 Remove lint and dirt from the inside.

2 Wash them by hand with a mild detergent.

3 Rinse.

4 Roll them in a towel to dry.

Lace

If your lace gloves are machine washable, place them in a mesh bag. Use a gentle cycle, mild detergent and warm water only. If they are too delicate for the washing machine, use the method described in 'Washing delicate items', below. Dry them by first rolling them in a towel, then laying them flat.

Washing delicate items

Small lace handkerchiefs and other delicate items that could be damaged by rubbing can be placed in a screw top jar filled with warm, soapy water. Soap flakes are fine. Shake vigorously. Rinse in clean warm water in the same manner.

To wash delicate net or chiffon, place the item inside a clean muslin bag first. Wash it in warm, soapy water (again, use soap flakes) and knead it gently. Rinse in the same fashion.

Starching

Stiffening fabrics with starch serves two purposes: it gives them body and crispness, and also creates an extra barrier to dirt. Starches are available in dry, liquid and spray forms, but you can also make them yourself. Some starches are applied during ironing; others can be put in the final rinse of the wash. Sprays are convenient when ironing or for a quick touch-up job on cuffs and collars.

To starch using liquids, dip clothes in the starching fluid after rinsing. Squeeze out excess water, hang the articles until nearly dry or roll in a dry cloth ready for damp ironing. Iron the garment on alternate sides until it is dry.

To stiffen synthetic fabrics, use sizings. These usually contain a cotton derivative, sodium carboxymethylcellulose, which stiffens when it is exposed to heat.

Drying

If you can, dry your washing outside in the fresh air: a clothes dryer consumes energy and costs you money while wet clothes over a clothes horse disperse a lot of extra moisture into the home, encouraging moulds and dust mites.

If you live in a flat or apartment, you don't have a clothes dryer and drying inside is the only option, use only one room if you can and keep a window open for ventilation. Shut the door of the room, sealing it off from the rest of the house. Of course, after several days of wet weather, especially if you live in a cold climate, you'll have no option but to hang damp clothes up to dry all over your home.

DRYING KNITS

If you have nowhere to dry a knitted top flat, run the legs of an old pair of pantihose (tights) through both sleeves and peg the waist and toes of the pantihose to the line. This technique helps support the weight of the garment and prevents peg marks.

Pegging out

Hanging clothes out is quite a simple task; however, if you follow these handy tips your clothes will last longer and ironing will be easier.

- Hang clothes straight away. If you leave wet clothes in the laundry basket, you risk colour runs and mould.

- Hang drip-dry clothes while they are dripping wet: they are designed to relax their wrinkles while drying.

- Lie knitted items flat in the shade.

- Place pleated garments in a stocking before hanging them up to dry. Roll them up if necessary.

- Dry white household linen and white clothing in the sun but coloured items and woollens out of the sun. The sun's bleaching effect is welcome on whites, but it can fade coloureds as well as shrink wool and cause white silk to yellow.

- Use plenty of pegs to support garments so they are less likely to be pulled out of shape.

- As a rule, peg the strongest part of the item — waistband, shoulders and toes, and the hems of t-shirts, dresses and shirts.

- Don't fold sheets before pegging them out as they will dry faster if allowed to billow between two lines. If you must fold them because you don't have enough line space, fold each sheet in four then refold and turn them from time to time to hasten drying.

Using a tumble dryer

Here are some tips for using your tumble dryer efficiently.

- Make sure your tumble dryer is vented to the outside so that the moist air is extracted.

- Use the washing machine's fastest spin option to squeeze as much water out of the load as possible. This will cut down the drying time.

- Sort the clothes first, grouping together items that need a similar drying time, otherwise you'll end up with some damp clothes and some that are over-dried and possibly damaged.

- Use the correct temperature for the fabric.

- Don't overload the dryer: the load should tumble freely. However, remember that drying full loads is more efficient.

- Reload the dryer while it's still warm from a previous load.

- Clean the dryer's lint screen after each load. Lint build-up limits air flow and so increases drying time.

- Do not tumble dry items that contain elastic or rubber.

Ironing

With so many easy-care, drip-dry clothes available these days, it's possible to avoid using an iron altogether, but there are still many people who regard a newly ironed, crisp cotton shirt as being worth the extra effort. And there are also some people who insist on ironing every item of washing, including towels and socks.

Ironing hints and tips

What you choose to iron is your choice, but when you do, here are some tips on how to go about it.

- First, dampen the clothes. Steam irons automatically dampen fabric as they iron, but some items will still benefit from dampening before ironing. The most effective way of doing this is to sprinkle the item with warm water, then roll it up tightly and put it aside. If you are really organized, you could sprinkle them and leave them in a plastic bag overnight. Alternatively, sprinkle the clothes an hour before ironing. Failing that, spray or sprinkle while you iron.

- Ironing brings out the best in a fabric, but it's important to follow a few basic rules. The iron must be hot enough to smooth a fabric's

SWEETLY PRESSED
Add a couple of drops of essential oil to a spray bottle of water, and use it to dampen clothing and linen when ironing.

Which iron setting?

FABRIC	IRON SETTING	DAMP OR DRY	WHICH SIDE?
Acrylic	Cool	Dry	Wrong
Cotton (dark)	Warm–hot	Either	Wrong
Cotton (pale)	Warm–hot	Either	Either
Linen (dark)	Warm	Damp	Wrong
Linen (pale)	Hot	Either	Either
Nylon	Cool	Damp	Either
Polyester	Cool	Damp	Either
Polyester mixes	Warm	Either	Either
Rayon	Warm	Damp	Wrong
Silk	Warm	Either	Wrong
Wool	Warm	Dry	Wrong

wrinkles, but not so hot that it damages it. Some fabrics should be ironed on the wrong side to avoid making them shiny, and others (such as wool) should not be ironed directly as this makes the fibres brittle.

- Unless the manufacturer specifically states that tap water is suitable for your iron, use either distilled water or demineralized tap water, both of which are available at supermarkets.

- Natural fabrics will simply burn if you iron them on too hot a temperature, but synthetic fibres may melt.

- Don't iron over plastic buttons and zips.

- Don't iron over metal objects that may scratch the plate.

- Use a pressing cloth over metal objects, especially when using an iron with a non-stick plate.

STERILIZE AS YOU IRON
A hot iron sterilizes tea towels and handkerchiefs.

Cleaning the iron

It's a good idea to keep the plate of your iron clean with this old-fashioned method: from time to time rub it with a cloth soaked in strong, cold tea, then wipe it with a soft, clean cloth. If you exercise some care when using your iron, you will avoid damaging the plate with melted fibres or rust. If something does go wrong, look at the table below for some cleaning and repair solutions.

How to iron clothes

1 First, iron thicker areas — such as collars, cuffs and waistbands — as these will wrinkle less while you complete the garment.

2 Next, iron structured areas that are not flat — for example, sleeves.

3 Finally, iron the flat areas such as shirt backs.

How to iron table linen

1 For a round tablecloth, start in the middle and work outwards.

2 Iron napkins flat. Do not iron in creases.

3 Iron damask, which is designed to be shiny, on the wrong side first, then on the right side.

Pressing

Knitted woollens and tailored items, such as suits, need pressing rather than ironing. This is best done professionally, but when that is not possible, or you want to touch up a garment, you can press at home.

To press, take a hot iron and a damp cloth made of calico or linen. Place the damp cloth on the garment and press heavily on the iron to remove creases. Continue pressing until the cloth is dry, but don't let it become singed. If the garment to be pressed is damp, do not dampen the cloth. Take care that the iron does not touch the garment itself or it may cause shiny patches.

How to clean a dirty iron

PROBLEM	SOLUTION
Accumulated brown stains	Rub the cold plate with a cut lemon
Clogged steam vents	Use a cotton wool bud and warm soapy water. If this doesn't work, pour white vinegar into the water tank and turn on the iron for a few minutes. Iron a clean rag to remove deposits. Cool and rinse with cold water
Dirty non-stick plates	Clean with a cloth dampened in warm water and detergent
Dirty ordinary plate	Rub with bicarbonate of soda and a damp cloth
Melted synthetic fibre	Heat the iron and gently scrape away large pieces with a wooden spoon or ice cream stick. Wearing an oven glove, remove smaller traces with cotton wool dipped in acetone (nail polish remover) and/or rubbing alcohol. If necessary, rub a regular plate with very fine steel wool, and a non-stick plate with a nylon mesh scrubber dipped in mild sudsy water
Plastic	Sprinkle some aluminium foil with salt and then iron it
Rust	Scour with salt and beeswax
Scratched surface	Rub with dampened salt and crumpled newspaper
Sticky plate (e.g. with starch)	1 Use a clean toothbrush. Heat the iron to warm and iron over a piece of waxed paper. 2 Clean with metal polish 3 While the iron is hot, run it back and forth over a sheet of clean paper that has been generously sprinkled with salt

IRONING LINEN

If you have hung linen to dry or laid it flat, once it is the correct dampness for ironing, roll it up tightly and place it in a plastic bag. Put it in the fridge or freezer if you do not intend to iron it within a couple of hours.

Bathroom

Bathrooms are utilitarian spaces, where we wash, put on our make-up and brush our teeth, as well as places where we find time for relaxation and indulgence — so they should be clean, fresh and well organized. In this chapter you'll find hundreds of handy hints on all aspects of bathroom management, including cleaning, storage, minor repairs, first aid and saving energy as well as some luscious homemade toiletry recipes.

Bathroom basics

- Steam and damp are present in the bathroom on a daily basis, so ventilation is important. Ventilation can be provided by gadgets such as a fan.

- Where possible, try to alleviate the pressure on a single toilet by installing another toilet elsewhere in the house, ideally with a small handbasin.

- Wall-hung items can make the bathroom seem more spacious because of the empty floor area.

- Large storage units can be subdivided into narrow shelves for smaller items and wider ones for bulkier things. Even within deep shelves you can section the space with baskets or boxes to keep smaller objects in order.

- Children's toys will be wet after playtime but can be rounded up in a nylon net bag or similar soft mesh container and left to drip dry over the bath or basin.

- Soap and sponges are often damp so should be kept on or in a holder that has a grill structure or a punched base so that the excess moisture flows away or evaporates.

- Wicker baskets are good for laundry and towels as they allow air to circulate around the fabrics inside, allowing any moisture to evaporate.

Bathroom safety

The combination of slippery surfaces and hot water in the bathroom can result in accidents, especially when young children or the elderly and frail are involved. To make your bathroom a safer place, take the following precautions.

- Never leave a young child alone in the bath. If the phone rings or someone knocks on the front door, either ignore the summons or take the child with you.

- If you have small children, never leave the bathroom door open when running the bath, or when there's water in the bath.

- Use shower curtains or screens to keep the floor as dry as possible.

- Avoid scalds by reducing your hot water temperature at the source or installing thermostatically-controlled mixer taps or fitting child-proof hot taps.

- Non-slip mats that adhere to the base of the bath are ideal for households with young children or older people.

- Install side grips and rails for extra stability near the toilet, bath and shower if a member of your household is elderly or infirm.

- Always keep medicines and cleaning agents out of reach of young children.

- Although glass and ceramic containers look attractive, they are not ideal materials as if they break they will leave sharp shards that are dangerous and can be difficult to remove.

- Angular corners and hard edges should be avoided on storage units and furniture as they can hurt unprotected skin.

The medicine cabinet

A well-stocked medicine cabinet and first aid kit are blessings, as it seems you need them most in an emergency or when it is difficult to get to a chemist. Remember that your cabinet should be child-proof, either locked or well up out of reach. If you are starting one from scratch, this list will help:

- Pain relievers and medicines to bring down fever (adult and junior versions if you have children in the house)

- Antiseptic cream

- Cotton wool buds

- Cotton wool balls, including a sterile pack

- Antacids for heartburn, stomach aches

- Anti-diarrhoea medicine
- Anti-itch cream
- Mild laxative
- Hydrocortisone cream for insect bites and eczema
- Bicarbonate of soda
- Petroleum jelly
- Cold/allergy remedy
- Antihistamine and decongestant
- Expectorant cough medicine
- Methylated spirits (denatured alcohol)
- Teaspoon or other dose measure, such as syringe, for children
- Hydrogen peroxide
- Syrup of ipecac
- Sunscreen
- Thermometer
- Family medical guide
- Hot water bottle
- Heat pack
- Ice pack (stored in your freezer)

TURN IT OFF
To save water, you should not leave the tap running while you brush your teeth — turn it on and off as needed.

FIRST AID KIT

A first aid kit comes in handy when you least expect to need it. Keep a kit in your car, as well as in the house. Pharmacists sell ready assembled kits; check against the following list and supplement where necessary.

- 1 small roller bandage
- 1 large roller bandage
- 1 small conforming bandage
- 1 large conforming bandage
- 2 eye pads with bandages
- Scissors
- Safety pins
- Calamine cream
- Pack of gauze swabs
- 2 triangular bandages
- Hypoallergenic tape
- 2 sterile pads
- Waterproof plasters or bandaids
- 1 finger bandage
- Tweezers
- 1 sterile dressing with bandage

Water-wise tips for the bathroom

The bathroom is the scene of many a water wastage crime: taps left on, long showers, deep baths, litres or gallons of water on its way to the sewage treatment plant every time the toilet is flushed. Whether you think this matters or not may depend on the source of your water: when it just keeps on coming out of the tap, you probably don't give it a second thought, but when you rely on a rainwater tank, for instance, the inconvenience of running out is often motivation to be more careful.

Shower

- Fit a low-flow shower rose. These use 7–12 litres (1½–2½ gallons) a minute of water, compared with up to 20 litres (4½ gallons) a minute with a standard shower rose.

- Alternatively, fit a flow restriction disc (a plastic insert) to your current shower rose.

- Have shorter showers. If you cut down from a 5 minute daily shower to a 3 minute one, you could save as much as 40 litres (8¾ gallons) of water per shower.

Toilet

- Flushing the toilet accounts for about one-third of an entire household's water use. Cisterns commonly contain 3–11 litres (½–2½ gallons) of water.

- Fit a dual flush system. New models use 6 litres (1⅓ gallons) for a full flush and 3 litres (½ gallons) for a half flush.

- For a single flush toilet, reduce the flushing volume by placing an old juice container full of water, or even a brick, in the cistern.

Cleaning and maintaining the bathroom

When giving the bathroom a good going-over, it makes hygienic sense to start with surfaces less likely to be contaminated with bacteria. Start by placing disinfectant in the toilet bowl and let it soak while you clean the

LIFE'S LITTLE LUXURIES

Essential oils Add a few drops of essential oil to a hot bath. Sage, lovage and orange are said to be stimulating, while lavender, mint, rosemary and marigold are relaxing.

Scented candles For an evening bath with a difference, light some candles in the bathroom and turn off the lights.

Bicarbonate of soda To soothe irritated and sunburnt skin, add bicarbonate of soda to your bath.

Epsom salts Add epsom salts to a warm bath or foot bath to ease swollen ankles and feet, and to relieve the early symptoms of a cold.

Bath bags For an alternative to bubble bath, gather a square of muslin into a little bag shape, fill it with flower petals or herbs, tie the bag and hang it over the taps as you fill the bath. Here are some simple ideas for the filling:

- Oatmeal and petals: Fill with oatmeal and petals of rose, lavender and chamomile.

- Fresh herbs: Fill the muslin with your favourite aromatic herbs, such as mint, lavender, rosemary and lemongrass. Either mix them together or use each one individually.

walls and floor, basin, bath and shower. Move on to the bidet if you have one, then the outer surfaces of the toilet, finishing with the inside of the toilet bowl.

Bacteria and other disease-causing organisms are often spread from hand to mouth after touching a contaminated surface. Therefore it is sensible to clean and disinfect door handles, the flushing handle and other places that are frequently touched after someone has been to the toilet.

All-round cleaners

There are several choices available for cleaning the basin, bath and outside of the toilet.

- **Commercial bathroom cleaner** A thick liquid, paste or powder containing bleach, abrasives and detergents with an overall acidic composition.

- **Mild detergent** A solution of dishwashing detergent is a good all-purpose cleaner for the bathroom and can be used on floors and walls as well as fittings.

- **Bicarbonate of soda** A mild abrasive which can be used as a general cleaner, or to remove tough spots. Can be used as a solution, a paste or powder.

- **Borax and lemon juice or vinegar** An all-purpose cleaner which keeps moulds at bay on shower curtains and other surfaces. A paste of borax and lemon juice left for half an hour will remove stubborn stains.

- **A solution of washing soda and water** This makes a tough, all-purpose cleaner.

- **White vinegar** Use with a brisk scrub.

- **Tea-tree** Diluted tea-tree oil keeps the brush and bowl germ-free.

Mould attack

Improving ventilation is the long-term solution, either by opening windows immediately after a steamy bath or shower, installing extractor fans, or fitting the room with wall vents so that steam and moisture can escape. Wiping away condensation will also help. Paint and grout is sometimes impregnated with fungicide.

Fresh as a daisy

To freshen the air in the bathroom and remove odours, make sure it has adequate ventilation. If necessary, open the window and try one of the following non-toxic air fresheners:

- Position ¼ cup white vinegar in an open bowl on a high shelf.

- Do the same with a bowl of clay-type cat litter.

- Make a simple spray air freshener for the bathroom by combining 1 teaspoon bicarbonate of soda and 1 teaspoon lemon juice in 2 cups hot water.

- Scented candles can help to banish bathroom smells, even if they're lit for only a short while.

- Lemon essential oil kills germs and is fragrant. Add a couple of drops to the final rinsing water when cleaning the bathroom.

- For an antiseptic air freshener, dissolve 1.25–2.5 ml (¼–½ teaspoon) of any antiseptic essential oil (thyme, bergamot, juniper, clove, lavender, peppermint, rosemary or eucalyptus) in 5 ml (1 teaspoon) methylated spirits (denatured alcohol), and then blend this with 500 ml (17 fl oz/2 cups) distilled water in a pump spray. Use your customized air freshener on the fine mist setting.

Cleaning walls and floors

Ceramic tiles are traditionally used for the floor and walls in the bathroom and have certain advantages for both surfaces. They are non-absorbent and do not deteriorate upon contact with water. While mould can grow on tiles, it is easily removed. Tiles are cold on the feet, but washable cotton mats remedy this.

Cleaning ceramic tiles

Frequent sweeping helps protect ceramic tile floors as well as keep them clean. Sand and grit, for instance, being harder than many glazes, can abrade glazed tile surfaces, causing them to become dull prematurely.

Washing removes dirt build-up. Use any non-acidic cleaner, with a gentle, or non-abrasive action. Detergent solution is fine. Use a toothbrush for hard to reach spots, including the grout between tiles. If you suspect the glaze is particularly delicate, closely observe whether a particular cleaner has dulled the surface. If it has, polish with a soft towel and avoid it in future.

No soap Do not use soap to clean ceramic tiles as it may leave a thin film of scum, which will gradually build up over time and can be difficult to remove.

Fixing a broken tile:

An important safety tip — as tiles splinter like glass does, always wear safety goggles, long sleeves and long pants to avoid injuries.

1 Using an old screwdriver, clean out the grout from around the tile. Scrape away until it's fairly clean. It doesn't have to be perfect at this stage.

2 Using the screwdriver and a hammer, gently tap away at the tile. Start from the crack, preferably in the middle of the tile. Never start at the grout line and work in. Always start in the middle and work out.

3 You can buy a 1-litre (35-fl oz) container of pre-mixed tile adhesive or you can even use silicone. If you do, keep it away from the edges so it doesn't squash into the grout lines. Next, tile in.

4 Mix up your grout until it has a consistency like toothpaste and grout away. Wipe off the excess.

The hand basin

A regular wipe-over with or without a cleaner, plus a weekly thorough going-over keeps the hand basin clean. Be sure to rinse the plug hole well to avoid leaving bathroom cleaner on it which could damage the coating. Scrub around taps and the plug hole with bicarbonate of soda to remove mould.

MOUTHWASH

For a safe and effective mouthwash, mix bicarbonate of soda with water and gargle with it.

OUT DAMNED SPOT

Mould and mildew Mix ¼ cup chlorine bleach in 2.5 litres (88 fl oz) of water. Scrub with a brush or toothbrush.

Limestone deposits Scrub with a little white vinegar and water, and rinse.

Blood Use hydrogen peroxide or household bleach.

Coffee, tea, food, fruit juice and lipstick Wash with detergent in hot water then hydrogen peroxide or household bleach. Rinse and dry.

Nail polish Wipe off with acetone, then, if necessary, use bleach.

Grease and oil Use an all-purpose cleaner.

Inks and dyes Steep the stain in household bleach until it disappears. Rinse and dry.

Chewing gum, wax and tar Chill with an ice cube then scrape away with a wooden spatula. Use paint stripper to remove any remaining trace.

Rust Use lemon juice in conjunction with mild detergent to remove stains such as rust on ceramic floor tiles. Squeeze lemon juice into a glass and add a few drops of dishwashing detergent. Cut an absorbent cloth into pieces the size of the stain and saturate them with the mixture. Place the cloth pieces onto the stain, wiping off any excess solution. Leave for a few hours. Repeat if necessary, then rinse with water.

Unblocking a sink

If you have a blocked sink, it's usually due to a build-up of grease or other matter in the trap. You could try using chemicals (proprietary drain cleaners), but if they don't work, try the following.

1 Take the trap off.

2 Disconnect the top and bottom, and clean out the trap. If the trap is clean, this means that the blockage will be further down the line, so you will need to call a plumber.

To clean taps

Wipe taps with chrome, plastic, gold and brass finishes regularly to remove traces of toothpaste and other toiletries. Clean with a solution of washing-up liquid or bicarbonate of soda, using a toothbrush for crevices.

TOYING ABOUT
Don't leave bath toys, sponges and loofahs in the bath where
they will remain almost constantly wet. To keep bacterial counts
down and prevent moulds from growing, let them dry out
between uses. Some people disinfect them between uses.
Choose toys that you can drain easily after a bath, wash regularly
and dry. Soak every now and then in a bleach solution.

To remove lime scale, wrap a cloth soaked in lime scale remover or
vinegar around the tap and leave according to the manufacturer's
instructions, or for up to half an hour.

The bath

Train the family to rinse the bath after they have used it. Leave a cloth
and light spray cleaner within easy reach so they can also wipe it over
regularly to keep soap and scum deposits at bay. An all-purpose
bathroom cleaner will do the trick: use a commercial one or your own,
made up into a solution and poured into a spray bottle.

Once a week or so, you'll need to do a more thorough clean, scrubbing
around the taps and plug hole and tackling any lime scale build-up.
Bicarbonate of soda is ideal for scrubbing around taps and plug holes,
while vinegar removes lime scale.

Warning

1 Do not use abrasive cleaners on acrylic baths as they may scratch.

2 Products designed to remove lime scale may cause enamel to dull. Try
   using a plastic scourer, neat washing up liquid and elbow grease.

Repairing the seals on the bath

The sealant around the edge of a bath will need to be repaired at some point
during the lifetime of the bath. Removing the old seal and replacing it with a
new one is a simple process, as follows:

1 Use a small paintbrush to apply a proprietary sealant-removal solution
   along the sealant bead. Allow this to soak into the sealant according to
   the manufacturer's guidelines.

2 Use a window scraper to ease the sealant away from the wall and bath surface, taking care not to scratch the surface of the bath.

3 Use a cloth to clean away any remaining sealant. Dampening the cloth with methylated spirits (denatured alcohol) will help to prepare the surface for reapplication of sealant to give a watertight finish.

The spa bath

It is important to follow the manufacturer's instructions on maintaining and cleaning your spa bath. You will probably need to clean out scum left in the pipe work, perhaps once a week. You can do this by filling the bath with warm water and a disinfecting agent, such as sterilizing tablets. Leave for 5 minutes. Empty the bath, then refill it. Turn on the spa and leave the water to circulate and rinse for another 5 minutes before emptying it.

The shower

Wipe over the floor of the shower recess with an all-purpose cleaner and use a lime scale remover as needed, perhaps once a week. Shower screens can be cleaned with a solution of washing-up liquid.

Cleaning a mouldy shower curtain If you have a problem with mould on your shower curtain, dry the curtain soon after showering. This will at least cut down on the amount of mould.

To clean mould from the curtain, you can use commercial mould removers but these often contain thickened chlorine bleach. Scrubbing with bicarbonate of soda is a less toxic alternative. Another method is to rub the curtain with a paste made with vinegar or lemon juice mixed with borax. Rinse well. Black stains are difficult to remove, but leaving the curtain to soak overnight in a weak bleach solution may help.

HOT AND STEAMY

To reduce the amount of steam produced when you run a bath or a spa, run the cold tap first, then the hot one. Less steam means reduced moisture and less chance of creating the warm, humid conditions in which fungi and moulds thrive.

Some shower curtains, especially nylon ones, are machine washable, but the plastic curtains are vulnerable to cracking so you should proceed with caution. Some shower curtains are impregnated with fungicides.

To clean dirty grout: You can buy products that whiten and kill moulds with fungicides. Alternatively, scrub with a solution of household bleach (1 part bleach to 4 parts water).

To clean sealant: To remove mould from sealant, wipe it with neat vinegar or rub over a paste of bicarbonate of soda. As a last resort, spray on a bleach solution (1 part bleach to 4 parts water) and leave it for 30 minutes. Scrub, then rinse clean with warm water.

Putting up a shower curtain rod

You can easily make your own shower curtain rod as follows:

1 Measure the width between walls, then buy and cut a piece of 20 mm (¾ inch) dowel that is 20 mm (¾ inch) shorter.

2 Put a screw into one end, leaving about 17 mm (⅔ inch) proud.

3 Find two pieces of rubber about 5 mm (¼ inch) thick. Glue one piece to one end of the dowel. Put the other piece between the wall and the screw. Adjust the screw until it fits tightly.

Fixing a dripping shower rose

The sideways spray from a shower rose is easily fixed by thread tape.

1 First unscrew the rose. Most modern roses have a washer — just replace it. Some are hinged and they leak right at the elbow. These also have a washer — replace it.

2 If it's leaking where there is just threaded pipe (like a bolt), thread tape is needed. Simply undo the fitting, expose the thread and wrap thread tape around it, probably about 10 times. Put the fitting back on the thread tape. The joins are now sealed.

The toilet

Toilet cleaners are at the harsh end of the cleaning scale in both environmental and health terms. Most are based on strong acids, such as sodium hydrogen sulphate. Other ingredients may include paradichlorobenzene (PDB), fragrance, detergent and bleach. These

NATURAL TOILET CLEANER

Take 1 cup borax and ¼ cup white vinegar or lemon juice. Mix the ingredients together and pour into the toilet bowl. Leave at least a few hours — overnight if possible — then scrub the bowl with a toilet brush. Add a few drops of pine oil to this recipe for extra disinfectant power.

Natural disinfectant

To make a disinfectant from essential oils, dissolve 20–30 drops of any oil with disinfectant properties — cinnamon, clove, pine, niaouli, tea-tree, thyme, bergamot, juniper, peppermint, rosemary or sandalwood — in 1 teaspoon methylated spirits (denatured alcohol). Mix with 4 cups distilled water and store in an airtight plastic or glass bottle.

chemicals should be used with caution as they can damage the skin and eyes; in addition, they do not readily break down.

Don't mix toilet cleaners Never use more than one toilet cleaner at a time, including bleach, as toxic gases may be produced.

All the outer surfaces of the toilet — rim of the bowl, seat, outside of the bowl — can be cleaned by wiping over with a solution of detergent or a cleaner of your choice. Clean the bowl with a toilet brush and disinfectant — either a commercial toilet cleaner or the gentler alternative above. To clean a toilet brush, hold it under the flushing water and rinse it in bleach.

How to unblock a toilet

If the pan is clogged and water is overflowing, turn off the water supply to the toilet. The tap is usually just behind the toilet.

1 First, wait a while to allow the water to subside — sometimes a blockage will clear of its own accord given enough time. If it doesn't, turn to the plumber's friend, the plunger. When using a plunger to unblock a toilet, some experts recommend a plunger with a metal disc above the rubber cup to prevent the cup turning inside out. Plunging requires more vigour for a toilet than a sink as there are no flat surfaces with which to make a good seal.

2 Wash the plunger by flushing the cistern while the plunger is still in the pan, then adding a little detergent and bleach to the pan water.

3 Depending on your confidence, or your skills, plumber's eels (jointed flexible tubing which can be pushed into drains to remove blockages) are a possibility, but it may just be simpler to call the plumber.

Fixing a leaking toilet

The cause of the leak is usually the flush cone — the large rubber washer which seals the pipe from the cistern to the pan. This eventually perishes, so check to see if yours looks cracked or dry.

1 Cut the flush cone with a Stanley knife and take it to the plumbing supply store to match it to a new one.

2 Cover the inside of the new cone with petroleum jelly and slide the small end over the flush pipe. Roll the big end of the cone backwards, turning it inside out. Get the flush pipe back into position inside the pan intake and place the large end of the cone forward. Wrap it around the pan intake in one hit.

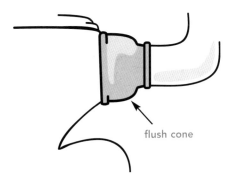

flush cone

3 Now simply massage it to adjust it.

Fixing a constantly running toilet 1

This problem is often caused by a worn cistern washer. It's a little difficult to fix, but worth a try.

1 Remove the lid of the cistern. Sometimes there's something stuck under the cistern washer, letting water out, such as an old blue toilet capsule or similar. Removing this may be all that's needed, but it's more likely that the washer has perished.

2 Turn the toilet off. (There is a tap behind the toilet which controls the flow of water.)

3 Flush the cistern to ensure you have a dry unit. At the bottom of the cistern, sealing off the entrance to the flush pipe, is a washer. Reach in and prise this off.

4 Take this washer to the plumbing supply store to match and replace it.

Fixing a constantly running toilet 2

If the problem isn't the toilet's cistern washer, then it could be due to the water intake washer.

1 Take the cistern lid off, push down on the float and listen for the water coming in. That is the water intake.

2 Turn the water to the toilet off and flush the toilet. This will ensure you have a dry unit.

3 Remove the float arm from the water intake — this is normally a plastic split pin or screw.

4 Unscrew the top of the water intake. There will be a washer in the top. As usual, with all plumbing fittings there are many different types, so it's best to take it to the plumbing supplier to match it and then replace.

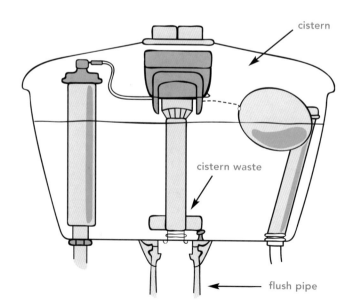

cistern

cistern waste

flush pipe

Replacing a toilet seat

The place to purchase a new toilet seat is at the plumbing supply store, as they will have the best range. To replace the seat:

1   Reach down under the back of the seat. On each side you will find a wing nut — this is a nut you can undo with your fingers. Unless your toilet seat is very old, these nuts will be plastic.

2   The new toilet seat will come complete with new screws and wing nuts.

NO-TEARS TIPS FOR TODDLER BATHTIME

It's common to experience problems with children not wanting to have their hair washed. You can make this experience fun by employing a few clever tactics as follows:

■ When it is hair-washing night, do the wash as soon as your child hops in the bath.

■ Swimming goggles can be put to good use at bathtime if your child's eyes are sensitive to shampoo suds. Have your child hold the goggles over her eyes while you use a plastic cup to rinse the shampoo out of her hair. Turn the event into a learning experience by counting each time you pour fresh water over her head, and encourage her to count, too. You might find it takes 20 cups of water or less to get rid of the suds. If you don't own goggles, substitute a face washer folded and pressed over her eyes, or shop around for special bathtime visors, which are stocked by pharmacists and some specialty shops.

■ With your help, let your child lather up the shampoo on her hair. This gives her some control over the situation and teaches her another skill that requires coordination.

■ Lather your child's hair so it pokes out in spikes, then give her a mirror so she can see the hilarious results!

■ Rinse her hair with an assortment of cups, bottles and even a watering can. Pretend your child is a flower, and every time her head is watered she grows just that little bit taller!

■ If your child still can't bear the thought of having her hair washed, the best option is to keep her hair quite short so the experience is quickly over and done with. For girls, at least, this strategy might be enough to coax them back into the bath!

Caring for towels

As bacteria love a moist environment, towels and face washers or flannels should be allowed to dry thoroughly between uses; on a sunny or windy day, it's best to dry them outside. Making sure each household member has his or her own towel will cut down the transfer of bacteria from one person to another.

As some toiletries contain substances that can damage towels and face washers or flannels, rinse them in cold water if they come into contact with, for instance, skin creams. Skin creams containing benzoyl peroxide can cause colour loss. Hair perming and neutralizing solutions are also particularly damaging.

Snip pulled threads on towels before they spread.

HOW HOT?

Children are more sensitive to hot water and usually prefer it at a maximum of 35°C (95°F), while babies are better off with bath water at 30°C (86°F).

- Hot water is 37–42°C (98.6–107.6°F).
- Warm water is 33–36°C (91.4–96.8°F).
- Cold water is 15–20°C (59–68°F).

Caring for brushes and combs

To clean brushes the old-fashioned way, dissolve a walnut-sized piece of washing soda in hot water in a basin. Comb out the hair from the brushes then dip them, bristles downward, into the water, keeping the backs and handles out of the water as much as possible. Repeat until the bristles seem clean. Rinse in a little cold water, shake well and wipe the handles and backs, but not the bristles, with a towel. Place in the sun or near a heater to dry. Do not use soap on bristles as this will soften them, as does wiping them.

Tortoiseshell or bone combs are best not washed, as water may split and roughen them. They should be cleaned with small brushes instead.

CHILDREN'S BUBBLE BATH

The children can help make this as long as a supervising adult deals with the boiling water.

Ingredients

4 tablespoons flower petals or heads (such as rose or lavender)

300 ml (10½ fl oz) bottle of baby shampoo

300 ml (10½ fl oz) boiling water

12 drops essential oil (such as lavender)

Method

1 Place the petals in a bowl, cover them with boiling water and leave for 15 minutes.

2 Strain the flower water into the other bowl.

3 Add shampoo and essential oil.

4 Pour the mixture into plastic bottles.

5 Shake each bottle for several minutes. Store any extra bottles that are not in use in a dark, cool place.

Bathroom recycling

- Cut hand towels and face washers from old towels and spruce them up with cheerful borders.

- Use old toothbrushes for cleaning jobs as well as for hobbies such as ceramics.

- Recycle chipped attractive mugs into tooth mugs but wash them regularly to avoid bacterial growth.

- Wash out a plastic bottle that has been used for soft drink or washing-up liquid and give it to the children to use as a bath toy: they'll have fun filling it up and pouring it out.

- Yoghurt pots and margarine tubs make excellent sorters for the medicine cabinet.

Homemade toiletries

If you've ever made your own homemade toiletries before, you'll know that they really work — and often smell glorious too. Here are some delicious recipes to try.

Egg shampoo

INGREDIENTS

1 egg
Hot water
Few drops liquid ammonia

METHOD

1 Separate the yolk from the white of a fresh egg.

2 Beat the yolk with a little hot water. Add a few drops of liquid ammonia for greasy hair.

3 Wet the hair thoroughly with hot water and rub the beaten yolk into the scalp.

4 Massage in for 2 or 3 minutes.

5 Rinse with soft hot water, gradually using cooler water.

Rose water and glycerine hand lotion

INGREDIENTS

150 ml (5 fl oz) rose water
100 ml (3½ fl oz) glycerine
1 drop pink or yellow food colouring

METHOD

1 Add the rose water and colouring to the glycerine little by little.

2 Mix together with a hand whisk.

Coconut honey cleansing cream

INGREDIENTS

70 ml (2¼ fl oz) coconut oil

1 tablespoon light olive or grapeseed oil

2 teaspoons distilled water

1½ teaspoons runny honey

10 drops essential oil of your choice

METHOD

1 Melt the coconut oil and olive or grapeseed oil in a double boiler until liquid (don't overheat). Remove from the heat.

2 Warm the water and honey to the same temperature as the oil. Slowly drizzle the water and honey into the oils, beating until no drops of water or honey can be seen.

3 Cool slightly and add essential oil, if you want. Beat to emulsify as the mixture cools. Pour into pots. Store in the refrigerator, as coconut oil becomes liquid at room temperature.

Rose water and witch-hazel

The following is a simple and effective toner for all skin types. If your skin is dry you can decrease the distilled witch-hazel and increase the rosewater. If you have oily skin you can do the reverse.

INGREDIENTS

100 ml (3½ fl oz) rosewater or hydrosol

30 ml (1 fl oz) distilled witch-hazel

½ teaspoon vegetable glycerine

METHOD

1 Mix all the ingredients together. Bottle them.

Papaya mask for oily skin

INGREDIENTS

Half a ripe papaya

1 tablespoon fuller's earth

1 tablespoon natural (plain) yoghurt

1 tablespoon orange blossom water

METHOD

1 Rub the pawpaw flesh through a sieve with a wooden spoon, then add the fuller's earth and yoghurt.

2 Mix thoroughly, then add the orange blossom water.

3 To use the mask, smooth it over your face and leave it for 15 minutes until it is almost dry. Break the mask up by rubbing your hands over your face then rinse with warm water. Finish with a cold splash.

Flower-infused cream

INGREDIENTS

175 g (6 oz) emulsifying wax

25 g (1 oz) dried flowers (such as marigold and rose petals)

75 g (2½ oz) glycerine

75 ml (2½ fl oz) water

METHOD

1 Melt emulsifying wax in a bowl over a saucepan of boiling water.

2 Remove the bowl from the heat and stir in the dried flowers, glycerine and water.

3 Place the bowl back on the pan and simmer for 3 hours.

4 Strain the cream through muslin placed over a sieve and squeeze out the excess liquid.

5 Allow to cool a little. Pour into sterilized dark glass jars.

6 Leave to set, tighten the lids and label. Keep refrigerated.

Simple scented cream

INGREDIENTS

50 ml (1½ fl oz) unscented base cream (available from chemists)

8 drops essential oil (e.g. lavender, chamomile, or a combination)

METHOD

1 Add the essential oil to the base cream.

2 Stir well. Keep refrigerated.

Eau de cologne

INGREDIENTS

150 ml (5 fl oz) vodka

50 ml (1½ fl oz) distilled or boiled water

60 drops orange essential oil

30 drops bergamot essential oil

30 drops lemon essential oil

6 drops neroli essential oil

6 drops rosemary essential oil

METHOD

1 Combine the vodka and oils in a bottle and leave for a week. Shake daily.

2 Add water, shake and set aside for 4 to 6 weeks.

3 Strain through a filter and funnel into a second sterilized bottle.

QUICK HONEY MASK

A simple honey mask is a stimulating cleanser for all skin types. It can be done very quickly, easily and cheaply. Spread some warm runny honey over your face and very gently begin to tap your skin with your fingertips until there is a feeling of 'pulling'. This takes about 2 minutes. Stop tapping and rinse your face well with coolish water. Blot dry.

bedroom

The bedroom should be comfortable and airy with a properly supportive bed covered in fresh bed linen, and all the drawers and wardrobe should be neatly stacked. If this doesn't sound like your bedroom but you'd like it to, this chapter will help, as it's filled with plenty of tips on cleaning, organizing and dealing with dust mites, as well as looking after clothes, shoes, jewellery, bags and luggage.

An ideal bedroom

- The ideal bedroom temperature should be around 18°C (64.4°F). Children and the elderly are particularly sensitive to temperature.

- The mattress has been manufactured for maximum back support.

- To protect against dust mites, the mattress and pillow are encased in microporous covers (for allergy sufferers only).

- Woollen or cotton bedding is best. It is less flammable than many synthetic fabrics, and also breathes, letting water vapour pass through.

- Clothes are well cared for, and hung and stored in such a way as to prolong their life. Old favourites are mended and patched; clothing which has lost favour is recycled or passed on to charity.

- Children's sleep wear is made from approved fire-safe fabric. To reduce fire hazards, most countries have strict standards relating to children's sleep wear: choose a fabric that is designated less flammable than others and a snug style that reduces the chance of clothing catching fire.

- If possible, locate your bedroom at the back or on the quietest side of the building, away from traffic noise.

- To ensure a quiet space, you may need to install double glazing, double doors or other forms of sound-proofing.

- If you have a window, it is pleasant to have it at the foot or side of the bed so that you can look out at the sky or view beyond, but avoid sleeping with your head directly under a window as you may be subjected to draughts of cold air while you are asleep which can cause stiffness in the neck and shoulders.

- Try to allow adequate space for the door to open and for the person entering the room to have a clear margin to turn around without walking into the bed.

Allergy alert: dust mites

Beds are breeding grounds for household dust mites. If you are sensitive to mites you may find that respiratory problems or even eczema rashes worsen at night. By trying some of the following, your symptoms may ease:

Bedclothes

- Bedding stored in divan drawers should be wrapped in breathable plastic bags to prevent dust mite droppings falling on them.

- An electric blanket keeps the bed dry, making it less inviting for mites and moulds.

- Avoid padded headboards, especially buttoned ones.

- Launder bedding frequently to reduce dust and kill dust mites. Experts recommend washing sheets, pillowcases and doona (duvet) covers weekly in hot water (56°C/132.8°F or above) to kill dust mites. If you prefer not to wash in hot water — perhaps for environmental reasons — or have bed linen which cannot be washed at 56°C (132.8°F), add a mite-killing chemical such as benzyl benzoate to the wash and give the linen an extra rinse.

- In hot climates, hang bedding in the sun for a few hours.

- Steam treatments kill mites near the surface but those deep inside mattresses and other soft furnishings remain unaffected. To be effective, the steam must be sufficiently hot for long enough not only to kill the dust mites but also to denature the allergen. Dead mites and allergen must be vacuumed afterwards. Carry out this treatment every 3 months or so.

- Doonas (duvets) are a better allergy option than blankets as you can put them in an anti-mite cover.

PUTTING THE FREEZE ON MITES
Place bedclothes, soft toys and favourite blankets in a chest freezer for a few hours, or overnight, to kill mites. You can then wash them out in warm, hot or cold water (or vacuum them if they're not washable).

Specialized anti-mite bedding

Barrier covers, designed to prevent you coming into contact with the mite allergen, are fitted over mattresses and pillows. The old-fashioned ones are made of plastic, which can make a night's sleep damp and uncomfortable as your body's sweat cannot pass through the cover. Modern covers are made from a soft, microporous material that allows water and air to permeate it. Covers that are impregnated with acaricide (a specialized pesticide which kills acarids such as mice and ticks) are also available to buy. When you buy anti-mite bedding, follow these tips:

- Buy a mattress with a guarantee.
- Make sure the cover fully encases the mattress, pillow and doona (duvet).
- Choose a water-permeable cover, to allow the fabric to 'breathe'.
- Don't buy a non-breathable type such as polyvinyl as it is uncomfortable.
- Check that the seams are double stitched for durability and have a good quality zipper.
- Buy a washable cover.
- Buy laminated covers rather than ones coated with polyurethane and polytetrafluroethane.

Reducing dust on furniture

- To reduce the amount of dust on furniture, keep the number of pieces in the bedroom to a minimum.
- Regularly vacuum under the bed.
- Damp-dust furniture and ornaments, and keep the tops of tall furniture free of dust.
- To make cleaning easier, choose easy-to-move pieces with a minimum of detailing.
- Keep the doors and drawers of wardrobes and chests closed.
- Remember that upholstered furniture encourages dust mites.

- Keep curtains dust-free by regularly vacuuming them or, if possible, washing them every 3 months at 56°C (132.8°F) or above.

Removing dust from flooring

- Consider removing the carpets and instead fit wooden floors (or another hard surface) and a washable rug.
- If you choose carpet, vacuum it thoroughly every week.

Ventilation and vapours

- Open windows, air blankets and the doona (duvet), and air the bed by pulling down the covers and leaving it for an hour or so before making the bed again.
- Do not hang newly dry-cleaned clothes in your bedroom.
- Do not smoke.
- Avoid using hairspray or other strong-smelling toiletries.
- Keep pets out of your bedroom.
- Be wary of new curtains, upholstery and floor finishes, all of which can out-gas chemicals.

The bed

Your bed should be neither too soft nor too hard. A slatted timber base with a quality mattress, such as a pocket sprung mattress made from natural fibres, or a futon, is recommended. Slatted wooden or metal bases provide better air circulation than divans; it is also easier to clean under a raised bed.

A divan bed has a base with a solid-sided frame, sometimes incorporating drawers and storage. It may be fitted with springs and padding, and be covered with fabric. The mattress sits on top.

Bedding

Today's typical well-dressed bed wears several layers of bed clothes. First, the mattress is protected by a mattress cover (which also provides some

BLANKET STITCH

When the edges of your blanket have frayed but the blanket itself still has life, trim any loose threads and use a thick woollen yarn to blanket stitch each side.

extra comfort) and a bottom sheet. Over the occupant lies a top sheet. For warmth, one or two blankets and/or a doona (duvet) are placed over the sheet. Both sheets are washable, and they prevent the other bedclothes from getting soiled or irritating the sleeper. A bedspread or cover protects the whole arrangement during the day.

Babies' bedrooms and bedding

Paradoxically, in preparing a room for a new baby, parents may introduce new hazards: new surfaces may include paints and varnishes, and curtains and carpets can emit numerous gases. Ensure there is excellent ventilation in a newly decorated room and try to finish it well before it needs to be used.

REDUCE THE RISK OF SIDS OR COT DEATH

Campaigns to reduce the risk of infants succumbing to SIDS (sudden infant death syndrome), or cot death, have focused on the following recommendations.

- Put your baby to sleep on his back.
- Do not cover your baby's head or face while he is sleeping.
- Place baby to sleep with his feet at the bottom of the cot.
- Tuck in the bedclothes securely.
- Do not use quilts, doonas (duvets), lambskins, pillows or cot bumpers in the cot.
- Do not use electric blankets, hot water bottles or wheat bags.
- Avoid smoking during pregnancy.
- Do not expose your baby to cigarette smoke, especially in his first year.

- When buying a cot, new or second-hand, make sure it meets the manufacturer's cot Standard for your country.

- The mattress should be firm and clean and exactly the right size for the cot — a baby can become trapped in gaps.

- The waterproof mattress protector must be a strong and tight fit.

Cleaning and care of clothes

Looking after the contents of your wardrobe means your clothes will always look their best and last longer. To prolong the life of clothes:

- Hang your jacket as soon as you take it off rather than sling it on the nearest object.

- Don't launder more often than necessary: if you wear a shirt for just an hour or so, hang it up to air and fasten the top, middle and bottom buttons before putting it back in the wardrobe. If necessary, spot-clean it rather than wash it.

- Dirt and sweat cause fabrics to deteriorate, so when clothes really need washing, do it sooner rather than later.

- When doing anything messy, protect clothes with an apron or overall.

- Use a scarf to protect the necks and collars of coats and jackets, especially leather ones, as hair and skin oils can stain.

Putting clothes away

Clothes need air to stay fresh. The cupboards, wardrobes and closets where you store your clothes should be dry and airy. Slatted shelves allow air to circulate: several shallow shelves are more effective than one or two deep ones and have the added benefit of making it easier to find items.

Don't be tempted to put even slightly damp clothes away. Wait until they are bone dry, as even the slightest touch of dampness will give clothes a musty smell that will be hard to remove.

For tailored jackets and skirts or trousers that you don't wash after each wear, air and brush them before putting them away.

PADDED HANGERS

Wide, shaped clothes hangers prolong the life of tailored clothing by spreading the weight and reducing the stress on the fabric. They also help preserve shape. Padded hangers are even better.

Hanging and folding clothing

Many items — jackets, trousers, skirts and dresses — should be hung up rather than folded and placed on a shelf or in a drawer.

Before you hang up your clothes, fasten zips and do up the top, middle and bottom buttons: this will help them to hold their shape. Empty the pockets, especially in wool garments that easily distort.

Hang trousers by the cuffs (the leg bottoms) or fold them over a hanger that has either a thick dowel bar or a paper guard to prevent a horizontal crease forming.

New life for old clothes

Patching, mending, cutting down and reusing clothes used to be a way of life. Nowadays we tend to throw out or give away a piece of clothing as soon as we're bored with it. But you can give clothing a new lease of life. Here are some ideas:

- **Dyeing** When the colours of a garment have faded but the fabric is not worn, dyeing — especially professional — revitalizes and smartens. This is also a good option for faded towels and bed linen.

- **Darning** Once darning socks was the norm, but these days cheap factory products have almost made it a redundant skill. Darning is still useful for repairing small holes that would otherwise make a woollen item unwearable.
  1. Take care to match the colour of the thread. If darning a patterned garment, using two colours may disguise the repair better.
  2. If possible, work on the wrong side.
  3. Take stitches well beyond the hole into the strong part of the fabric.

- **Patching** This repair method is ideal for children's play clothes and also useful for adults' clothes that can take a bit of character — for example, elbow patches on a comfortable tweed jacket or favourite woolly jumper. Circular or diamond patches wear better and show less than squares and rectangles. Choose soft supple leather for elbow patches and for strips along the end of a sleeve or along the front of a pocket. Cut a generous size that amply covers worn areas with plenty of margin. Use a blanket stitch or buttonhole stitch with a little slack to allow for movement. Use button thread.

- **Shortening** Trousers with holes at or below the knee can become gardening shorts.

- **New buttons** New trims and buttons dress up and contemporize.

- **Fancy dress** Eccentric hats, uncomfortable but glamorous shoes and other purchasing mistakes, especially ones made from unusual fabrics, make desirable items in a children's dress-up box.

- **The cover up** Big old shirts are ideal for dirty work like cleaning, hobbies and gardening.

- **Odd socks** Odd or old socks are useful for storing safety goggles, as ladder end pads and for various jobs around the house, including polishing.

- **Pyjama legs** If not too worn, these can be secured in place over ironing boards.

Common clothing repairs

- **To mend an L-shaped tear** When clothes catch and tear on a sharp object, pull the edges together and tack them to a piece of finely woven cloth on the wrong side of the fabric. Using threads from the garment, if possible, make a series of diagonal stitches across the tear in one direction, then in the opposite way so they form a trellis pattern.

- **Pockets** A worn pocket is a liability and an unnecessary one at that. For holes in trouser pockets, cut off the worn area and sew in a new piece in a tough fabric such as drill or calico. Alternatively

BASIC SEWING KIT

Even if all you do is sew on loose buttons, every house deserves a small repair kit.

- **Scissors** A small pair with sharp points for cutting thread; dressmaking shears if you plan to tackle fabric.

- **Needles** A range is best, according to likely tasks: ordinary, embroidery, darners, upholstery.

- **Thimble** Protects the middle finger when pushing a needle through fabric.

- **Threads** White, black and beige are a good base.

- **Pins, tape measure and fastenings** Include a button collection.

you could fit an entirely new pocket — these are available ready-made if you don't want to start from scratch. To fix patch pockets that have ripped from the back, unpick the top corners, and place a strip of cotton behind the tear or weak area. Fix it with running stitches then lightly darn on the right side. Finally, reattach the pocket firmly.

Storing clothes

Before putting clothes away for long-term storage, or to store until next season, make sure you follow this check list.

- Do wash or dry-clean them. Dirt is more likely to attract pests such as insects, and encourage mildew.

FRESH AIR
- To add a fresh smell to your wardrobe or chest of drawers, place a couple of teaspoons of pot pourri or dried lavender in a piece of lightweight fabric such as muslin or cheesecloth and tie with a ribbon.
- To remove the smell of moth balls: scrub with equal parts white vinegar and lemon juice. Repeat if necessary.

WRINKLE LESS
When you are packing a suitcase or putting away valuable clothes, placing tissue paper (acid-free for storage) between fabric layers with the garments themselves helps reduce creasing and wrinkling.

- Do air items, especially ones you've steam-ironed or damped down before ironing.

- Do use muslin or canvas storage bags, or clean white or undyed sheets.

- Do place items on wire racks rather than shelves to allow air to circulate properly.

- Don't starch items to be stored as starch attracts meal-seeking silverfish, which do not discriminate between the starch and the clothing fibre.

- Don't store clothes in dry-cleaning plastic or other garment bags that do not breathe as moisture may be trapped inside. In addition, dry-cleaning bag plastic may cause yellow streaks over time due to plasticizers.

- Don't put clothes or shoes away while they are still damp.

Moths

The webbing clothes moth (*Tineola bisselliella*) is the most common fabric moth. It is particularly attracted to wool and furs, and its larvae eat the fibres, leaving a rash of holes. Stored, unused clothing is most vulnerable as moths do not attack clothes that are in constant use. Regular airing and shaking does much to guard against moth attack. Pockets should be turned out and fluff brushed off.

Rid clothes of insects by washing in hot water, 50–60°C (122–140°F), or by dry-cleaning. It is important to do this before storing the clothes.

Commercial moth treatments are not only toxic to moths, but also to humans. They include naphthalene and PDB (paradichlorobenzene), which is an organochlorine. These treatments kill moths, larvae and eggs in an airtight situation where they saturate the insects. If you must resort to these, they are best used only in spaces that are not living areas, such as attics or garages.

Natural moth treatments

- If you suspect moths have invaded an article of your clothing, wrap it in a clean, damp towel, and put it in a low oven to steam out the grubs, or place it underneath a damp towel and press it with a hot iron.

- If you can actually see moths, brush the article with a solution of 3 tablespoons turpentine and 2.8 litres (98 fl oz) water.

- To defend drawers and cupboards from moth invasion, keep them free from dust and fluff by regularly airing and vacuuming them. Wipe over with a repellent such as eucalyptus oil.

- Cotton wool buds dipped in essential oils are said to keep moths away from clothing. You could try lavender, lemongrass, camphor or rosemary and place a couple in each drawer between your items of clothing. Or dot a few drops of essential oil on sheets of blotting paper, fix the scent with orris root powder and use them as drawer liners.

- Herbal deterrents include sachets of cedar chips, dried lavender flowers, dried rosemary or southernwood. Place these among your clothes, where they not only help to deter moths and silverfish, they also keep clothes smelling fresh.

- Line drawers with brown paper, butcher's paper or wallpaper off-cuts. Scatter herbal repellents underneath the paper.

- Make sachets from light fabrics such as muslin and fill them with a mixture of ground cloves, nutmeg, mace, caraway seeds, cinnamon (30 g or 1 oz each) and orris root powder (90 g/3½ oz). This amount of mixture will fill several sachets.

- If these treatments cause irritation you may need to store moth-vulnerable clothing in sealed plastic bags.

Cleaning and care of shoes

- Shoes will last longer if given a day's rest after wearing to allow moisture to evaporate, so have at least two pairs for each season.

- Keep your shoes on shoe trees when not in use to keep the shape and avoid cracking.

- Caring for the leather helps prevent cracks developing.

- Use a hard brush to remove mud; never scrape with a knife.

- Repair damaged shoes as soon as they need it. Delaying repair is a false economy.

To soften leather

- Rub with lemon juice or castor oil. Olive oil helps prevent the leather from cracking and drying.

- To help wear in new shoes, carefully pour a small amount of methylated spirits (denatured alcohol) into the shoes at the heels and let it soak in. Wear the shoes while still wet.

- Where a shoe pinches over a toe or joint, press a very hot damp cloth over the spot, and leave it for a few minutes so that it expands and softens the leather.

Removing stains on shoes

Always proceed with caution, especially for pale-coloured footwear.

- **Grease stains on leather** Daub with petrol then egg white.

- **Grease stains on suede** Rub with rag dipped in glycerine.

- **Tar** Remove with petrol.

- **Other stains** Sponge with a solution of warm water and vinegar. Polish when dry with a soft cloth soaked in linseed oil. Remove all traces of the oil with a soft, clean cloth.

Drying shoes

Leather that remains wet can become irreversibly damaged; drying wet shoes too quickly can cause cracking.

TO DEODORIZE SHOES
Sprinkle bicarbonate of soda inside. Leave for a day or two, then shake out and air.

- Never dry shoes in front of a fire or heater.
- Stuff shoes with balls of newspaper or sand — the latter dries them quickly without altering their shape.
- Fine leather shoes can be revived after a dousing if you coat them in oil or petroleum jelly. Boots and tougher shoes can be rubbed down with saddle soap.
- To polish leather that is a little damp, first rub over with a cloth to which a few drops of kerosene have been added.

Storing shoes

The best shoe treatment consists of using shoe trees to keep them straight. If you store shoes for a long period, put them in individual shoe bags or wrap them in tissue paper.

Caring for jewellery

A little bit of knowledge goes a long way when looking after jewels.

- Do store precious jewels in padded boxes or bags to protect against sunlight, dust and humidity.
- Do avoid extremes of temperature.
- Do keep precious pieces separate from each other to protect against scratches and tangles.
- Do take extra care cleaning jewellery with loose stones as the dirt may be all that is holding them in place.
- Do take the gentler options first when cleaning, starting with a soft brush such as a paint or make-up brush on very dusty pieces.
- Do take valuable pieces to professionals for cleaning if you are in the slightest doubt about how to go about it yourself.

- Don't spray accidentally with hairspray or perfume as these can dull some surfaces.

- Don't use any substance on jewellery without being absolutely sure it is recommended for all the materials the jewel is made from. This includes water, detergent, ammonia, bicarbonate of soda and jewellery cleaning cloths and dips.

How to wash jewellery

A lot of jewellery can be washed in a mild detergent and water solution, and gently brushed with soft bristles, but stones set with glue should not be washed. While transparent gems such as diamonds, sapphire and ruby are hard and do not absorb water, opaque gems such as opal, amber and so on should be wiped only with a damp cloth then patted dry.

Hard water can leave a chalky residue on precious stones. If you live in a hard water area, clean with distilled water.

Never clean jewellery in the sink as you risk losing pieces down the drain should they come apart. Use a bowl instead.

Once you are sure a jewel can be washed, proceed as follows:

1 Put some water and some washing up liquid into a small bowl: hot water (not boiling) is fine for diamonds, otherwise use lukewarm water.

2 Soak for 15 minutes to loosen the dirt.

3 Rinse.

4 With a small, soft brush — for instance, a baby's toothbrush or a paintbrush — work detergent into the crevices.

5 Rinse and dry on a lint-free cloth such as a tea towel.

DO NOT WASH

The following substances are relatively soft and may absorb not only water but also chemicals, including soap or other cleaners.

- Amber
- Bone
- Coral
- Ivory
- Lapis lazuli
- Malachite
- Mother-of-pearl
- Opal
- Shells
- Turquoise

Caring for pearls

Wearing pearls often is said to be the best way to care for them, as the oils in your skin give them a gentle lustre.

- Do not wrap pearls in cotton or wool as the extra heat this generates can dry them out and cause cracking.

- Dampen pearls from time to time in lightly salted water.

- After wearing pearls, wipe them with a soft cloth or chamois leather, dry or damp, to remove traces of perspiration, which, being acidic, can damage the pearl surface.

- If your pearls are really dirty, you can wash them in water and a very mild soap, then clean them with a soft cloth. Lay them on a moist tea towel to dry. The pearls will be dry at the same time as the towel.

Caring for wooden beads, bangles and brooches

Wipe with a damp chamois cloth and rub well with a little olive oil. Finally, buff with a soft cloth.

Caring for glass beads

Shake glass beads in a plastic bag with 2 tablespoons bicarbonate of soda. Dust with a soft brush and buff with a damp chamois cloth.

Leather bags and luggage

Before cleaning an item of luggage, check the manufacturer's care label as both leather and suede are available in two different types — one can be washed but the other should be dry-cleaned. Use different methods of cleaning for different types of leather.

- Brush suede with a suede brush or an off-cut of suede.

- Finish leather with wax polish to keep it supple.

- Smear petroleum jelly on patent leather then buff it dry.

- Rub leather bags over with neat's-foot oil from time to time, or polish with boot polish.

● To renovate an old leather bag, use a warm, not hot, solution of washing soda to remove grease and dirt. Apply it with a soft rag or a brush if it is very dirty. Oxalic acid, used after the soda, may remove stains. After cleaning, wash with lukewarm water, place in a warm spot to dry and once dry, treat with a wax polish.

A FRAGRANT BEDROOM

■ Herb and lavender pot-pourri

Ingredients

1 cup lavender flowers
½ cup dried spearmint
½ cup dried marjoram
½ cup dried oregano flowers
2 tablespoons powdered orris root
2 tablespoons lavender essential oil

Method

Mix the ingredients together well, then place the mixture in a plastic bag for 2 weeks to mature. Shake the bag regularly. Transfer the pot-pourri to an ornamental bowl.

■ Lavender bag

Put lavender sachets or bags in a drawer to prevent their contents from becoming musty. This bag will retain its scent longer if you keep the stalks on.

Ingredients

lavender in full bloom
newspaper
muslin or fine cotton
ribbon

Method

Cut the lavender and spread the stems out to dry on newspaper, either in the sun or in another warm place. Cut the fabric to the size and shape required and stitch into a simple bag shape. When the lavender is dry, insert a bunch into the bag so that the stems stick out of the opening. Close the opening with hand stitching or a length of ribbon. Trim the stalks to a length of 5 cm (2 inches).

 # index